KEEPING IT BRIEF

Volume 1

Short Daily Devotions to Draw You Closer to God

CHERYL PHILLIP-JORDAN

Bladensburg, MD

Keeping It Brief Volume 1

Published by Inscript Books
a division of Dove Christian Publishers
P.O. Box 611
Bladensburg, MD 20710-0611
www.dovechristianpublishers.com

Copyright © 2021 by Cheryl Phillip-Jordan

Cover Design by Mark Yearnings

All rights reserved. No part of this publication may be used or reproduced without permission of the publisher, except for brief quotes for scholarly use, reviews or articles.

Scripture quotations are from the King James Version of the Bible (public domain).

ISBN: 978-1-7359529-4-9

Printed in the United States of America

Contents

Preface	viii
Acknowledgements	ix
At a Distance	1
Logic	3
A Prayer of Return	4
Treasure	5
Sing Praises	7
Shelter in Place	9
Great is the Lord	11
Higher	12
Forever life	13
Think	14
Consultations	15
Sufficient	16
Our Source for Help	17
Anointed for a Purpose	18
Food	20
Naaman	22
Race	24
Preparation	25
Legacy	26
Altars	28
Speak Right	30
Glory Belongs to Him	31
The Love of God	33

Light and Sound	34
Siege	35
Clear the Channel	36
Substitute	38
Be Ready	40
The Crowd	42
Universal Praise	43
Final	44
Camera	45
Hedge	46
Sent by God	47
Just Imagine	49
One Touch	50
Fight	51
This Time Tomorrow	53
Goodness of God	55
Harvest	56
Different Paths	58
Make Room	59
It Seems Right	61
Declaration	62
On Your Side	63
In Joseph's Position	64
Enemies	65
Response	66
Knowledge	67
Dwelling Place	68

The Lord Himself	69
Don't Compound It	70
Steps to Victory	71
Influence	73
Giants	74
Concern for others	75
Blessed by Association	76
Children	78
Waiting Required	79
Nehemiah	81
Skip to the Good Part	83
Still He Loves Us	85
Inner Cleansing Required	86
Decision Time	88
The Talking Donkey	89
God of Abundance	91
Deliverance	92
Precious Life	93
Lies, Lies	94
Well Done	96
In the Furnace	97
Always Done	99
On the Inside	100
The Change	101
The Homecoming	102
Life Storms	103
The Thief	105

Revealing	106
War or Rest	107
For Want of Ten	109
Kingdom Training and Preparation	110
To Make Great	112
Praise in the Wilderness	113
Eagle or Grasshopper	115
Please Him	116
Hearts are Set	117
Our Hope	118
A Perfect Heart	120
Prophet, Priest, and King	121
The Choice	122
Restoration	123
Priority	125
Bring the Book	126
No More Delays	127
Our Father Abraham	129
The Real Trouble	130
Determination	131
Eyes Right	133
No Other	134
Nehemiah, the Wall Builder	135
Think Again	137
Filled	139
Bread in the Wilderness	140
Water	141

A Different God	142
King Uzziah	143
The Setback	145
Still Blessed	147
Not the Same	148
King Saul	149
Just Great	151
Reasons Why?	152
Impact	154
The Inside Enemy	155
Tune In	157
Manna	158
Instruction	159
Promotion	160
Noah	162
Naturally Different	163
His Plan	164
Dilemma	165
End Well	166
A Time to Run	168
The Challenge	169

Preface

This is a collection of daily devotionals which, if read each morning, will last for about four months. These short pieces are all based on the Word of God and will encourage, inspire, educate, and promote interest in His Word. God's Word is unlike the word of human beings. It is always true, alive, powerful and lasts forever.

As we lead our busy and not-so-busy lives, we cannot afford to bypass the important principles laid down in His Word. Many of our misfortunes are caused by our lack of knowledge of His Word or by our failures to apply 'head' knowledge to practical everyday life.

God never intended that we develop only academic interest in Him and His Word. He desires involvement in our day-to-day activities, even though we seem to believe He belongs only within the walls of places of worship and is relevant only at particular times of the year or when we are in trouble.

Through discouragement, disappointment, misfortune, or in times of great blessings, the Word of God remains relevant, teaching, guiding, strengthening, and upholding us. As you read and meditate on the daily pieces, be aware of His loving arms, all-seeing eyes, sensitive ears, and caring heart. He deserves our attention, our praise, and our worship.

Love Him completely, because He loves us more than we understand.

Acknowledgements

Thank you, Holy Spirit.

I wish to thank my husband, Edgar Jordan, whose support and encouragement remained constant throughout this project. My daughter, Kamaria, provided invaluable assistance in typing and editing.

Thanks to my pastor, Rev. Dr. Melch Pope, under whose teaching I developed a greater appreciation and love for the Word of God.

Rev. Michael Alleng and Pastor Ricardo Yarde, both of whom I lovingly refer to as my 'away pastors,' guided me through an important spiritual journey, without which this project would never even have started. It was the suggestion of Rev. Alleng, that these pieces be combined in a single publication. Thank you.

To the many others who offered assistance and prayer, made suggestions, gave feedback, provided encouragement and otherwise, I say thanks.

Thanks to you, dear reader. Be blessed!

1

At a Distance

A new term has become part of our everyday language since the COVID-19 virus entered our landscape. That term is *social distancing*. It refers to the practice of maintaining space between ourselves and others so that we do not get close enough to anyone to encourage the spread of the virus. Social distancing is beneficial, as it has proved effective in slowing down the transmission of the virus from one person to another.

However, it seems that some of us have been practising 'spiritual distancing' for some time now. At least, we have tried. Some of us have been deliberately distancing ourselves from our brethren, and we have also tried to even put enough space between ourselves and God. We do not want Him so close that He influences every aspect of our lives, but we choose to maintain a distance. We want Him nearby where we can call Him whenever there is a problem but at a distance when everything is going well.

In the face of this current crisis, let us draw closer to Him. There are no other viable options on the table. It was never in the plan of God that we pull away from Him and try to distance ourselves from His presence, from His power, and from His purpose for our lives.

- *"But the word is very nigh unto thee, in thy mouth, and in thy heart, that thou mayest do it."* (Deuteronomy 30:14)

- *"In the beginning was the Word, and the Word*

was with God, and the Word was God." (John 1:1)

- *"And the Word was made flesh, and dwelt among us."* (John 1:14)
- *"Draw nigh to God, and he will draw nigh to you."* (James 4:8).

As we draw closer to Him, we will inevitably draw closer to each other.

The choice is ours. What are we going to do?

2

Logic

Some things, like micro-organisms, can be seen if examined with the right instrument.

Other things cannot be seen, regardless of the instrument: wind, gas, gravity, temperature, and electricity.

So they are fictitious and cannot be real?

Well, we can't see God either (John 4:24).

3

A Prayer of Return

Luke 15:11-24

I wandered away
Far from the Lord
I spent a long time
Thought I was enjoying myself
Now things have changed
And I realise
I need to return to my Father
Will He still love me?
Will He still have me?
My Father, forgive me
Oh Father!
Now I understand
Now I appreciate
Your love
Your kindness
Your goodness
Thank you, Father
I want to be with you
Forever!

4

Treasure

What do we value most in our lives? That will bring different responses from different persons.

Is it our money, successful business ventures, bank accounts, and all the privileges they bring?

Some of us put our careers, homes, vehicles, clothes, jewellery, and other possessions as being the most important things in our lives.

Some treasure giftings and abilities or country of residence; others, their education.

A few of us have had the fortune to be born into a family that is well-connected. We carry a name that is easily recognised in society.

Now, we have a lot of time for reflection. Most of us have had our busy lives screech to a halt or at least, slowed down.

This is the acid test. Is whoever or whatever we have been trusting in, able to provide relief and assurance at this time?

Educated or not, wealthy or not, held in high esteem or not, we were all created by Him (Genesis 1:27) and need to place our treasure in Him.

At the end of the day, that is the only safe place (Matthew 6:21). Since we are His treasure (Exodus 19:5), should not the relationship work the other way as well?

It is time for self-evaluation and examination. It is time to trust Him as never before.

It is time to love the Lord and serve Him with all our heart and all our might (Deuteronomy 6:5), not only in this crisis, but always.

For this time of trouble will last for a while and then be over, but He remains eternal.

5

Sing Praises

Nothing seemed to be looking up for Paul and Silas. They were in the will of God, doing His work, spreading His Word, when they fell victim to ungodly forces (Acts 16:16-24). Berated, beaten, bloodied, and bound, they were locked up in the inner prison. They had good cause to sulk, grumble, murmur, and complain. But in their darkest hour, they sang praises, not in their hearts, but loudly, so that other prisoners heard them (Acts 16:25).

What did their fellow prisoners think? *Surely these men are insane, stupid, or simply do not grasp the gravity of their situation.* But victory came as they praised. There was a great shaking, doors were opened, and there was liberty. The prison keeper and his family came to the Lord. Official freedom for Paul and Silas came in the morning.

In our current situation, many of us feel imprisoned in our homes. We have taken a financial beating, an emotional beating, or even a spiritual beating. There are falling incomes and scary happenings, while we are cut off from physical contact with our friends and unable to attend the House of God. We may feel insecure and abandoned.

However, singing praises is the way to go. It not only lifts our spirits but also the spirits of those around us, or at least, it gets their attention. Even more importantly, it invites the presence of God into our situation. Nothing and no one remain the same in His presence.

Think of something that God did in your life and sing praises.

Commit the future to Him and sing praises.

Those in your household will hear your praise.

- Praises invite His presence *(**Psalm 22:3**)*
- Praises bring relief *(**Psalm 18:3**)*
- Praises bring victory *(**2 Chronicles 20:22**)*

Regardless of our frame of mind (Psalm 108:1; Psalm 42:11; James 5:13), praises are desirable.

As we praise, doors open or new opportunities present themselves, souls are won to the Kingdom and we are set free.

6

Shelter in Place

In these pandemic times, this phrase is often used. It is advised to remain where you are, once it is a safe place, until the danger is passed.

We, the people of God, have also been called to remain under our Lord's protection.

Noah and his family sheltered in place in the ark. He had answered the call to build the ark (Genesis 6:14). His family was saved from destruction. After Noah, his family, and the animals entered the ark, the door was shut by God Himself (Genesis 7:16). There was no turning back.

The children of Israel sheltered in place in Egypt, on the night of the first Passover. They were instructed to remain in their houses (Exodus 12:22).

King David was an expert at sheltering in place. His many experiences at being on the run, in fear for his life, saw him frequently hiding (1 Samuel 22:1; 24:22; 26:1). He recognised that more than just a physical hiding place was needed (Psalm 119:114).

The prophet Isaiah urged God's people to shelter in place to escape His judgement (Isaiah 26:20).

The apostle Paul advised the centurion and his soldiers to shelter in place, even as they prepared to abandon ship in the middle of a storm (Acts 27:31).

We are to remain in Him, in safety under His blood. There is no other refuge, no other safe zone. Let us shelter in place, for our adversary the devil, is roaming around, seeking someone to devour (1 Peter 5:8).

No one shelters in place when there is no trouble. This command is only issued when danger lurks outside.

The climate of this pandemic can easily steal our peace, our stability, and our mental health. Let us remain in the safety and security provided by Him. We are not to simply confine ourselves to our homes, but we are to secure our hearts and minds in Him, for there we find hope, peace, joy, and strength (Nehemiah 8:10; Psalm 29:11; Romans 15:13).

7

Great is the Lord

*"Great is the L*ORD*, and greatly to be praised; and his greatness is unsearchable."* Psalm 145:3

His greatness is unsearchable.

- It cannot be analysed.
- It cannot be understood.
- It cannot be duplicated.
- It cannot be substituted.

If His greatness lay within our reasoning, then maybe we could come up with alternatives. We would seek to place His greatness alongside that of others in the realm of the natural and in the realm of the spiritual.

But as it stands, His greatness far exceeds that of any human being, any spiritual being, any organisation, or any nation.

Who wouldn't want to serve this God?

Great is the LORD!

8

Higher

"For as the heavens are higher than the earth, so are my ways higher than your ways, and my thoughts than your thoughts." Isaiah 55:9

The heavens are not just a couple miles above the earth, or a couple hundred miles; they are completely out of our reach. True, we have landed on the moon, sent probes to other planets and our telescopes are sending back pictures of parts of the heavens, but that is just a drop in the bucket.

The distance, vastness, and extent of the heavens are impossible to calculate or to imagine.

Our planet, Earth, is just a small part of our solar system, which itself is just a small part of our galaxy. The Milky Way, our galaxy, is simply one of billions in the heavens that we can see. The heavens are infinite and limitless. Imagine the God who created them!

He, *"stretcheth out the heavens as a curtain, and spreadeth them out as a tent to dwell in."* Isaiah 40:22.

It stands to reason, that the God who created the heavens, must be bigger and more complex than His creation. Yet, He loves us and wants to have a personal relationship with us.

If you have not yet made Him your Lord, this is a great time to do so.

Lord, I repent of all my sins. Please forgive me. I want to serve You for the rest of my life, in Jesus' name. Amen.

9

Forever life

Some believe that they and their memory will live forever if they have streets, towns, and facilities named after them.

Others believe that monuments erected in prominent city spots will ensure a memory that never dies.

Others surmise that many sons and grandsons ensure the family name, and consequently, they live on for many generations.

The fact is that we are all going to live forever whether we achieve any of the above. The only question is the place where that eternal life will be spent.

We can accept Jesus and ensure a heavenly home (Acts 16:31; Luke 23:43).

OR...

We can refuse to accept Him and spend an unpleasant eternity in Hell (Mark 16:16).

Only two options exist. It is a clean cut-and-dry choice. There is no middle ground. To refuse or neglect to accept is to reject.

Today we choose. Tomorrow may be too late.

10

Think

"Finally, brethren, whatsoever things are true, whatsoever things are honest, whatsoever things are just, whatsoever things are pure, whatsoever things are lovely, whatsoever things are of good report; if there be any virtue, and if there be any praise, think on these things."
Philippians 4:8

The apostle Paul was not in a luxury hotel or relaxing at home when he wrote these words. He was in prison unjustly. Yet his writing is full of joy and the spirit of rejoicing.

What kind of thoughts are dominating our minds in these troubling times? We may be thinking of loss, of separation, of an uncertain future, and even of the good old days; those good old days when we criticised the same things for which we now yearn. How times have changed!

Let us focus though on pleasant things and let us not allow our minds to wander aimlessly, for if we do, it tends to settle on the undesirable.

Focus on Him, His love, His goodness, and His soon return.

11

Consultations

Though it is socially acceptable and even fashionable to consult with those who have familiar spirits (clairvoyants, psychics, palm readers, sorcerers, and the like), God is still against it (Acts 13:6-12).

It does not matter if what they are saying is true (Acts 16:16-18), the Lord commands His people to stay away from them (Deuteronomy 18:10-12).

12

Sufficient

In the Old Testament, the Syrians thought the power of God was restricted to the hills (1 Kings 20:23-29). God knew their reasoning and heard their conclusion. He showed them their thinking was flawed when they were defeated by God's people on the plains.

The idea of a god with limited power was not strange to them. That would explain the need for multiple gods, if every god is powerful in restricted times, places and situations.

But our God is one God (Deuteronomy 6:4; Ephesians 4:6) and since He has:

- all power (Jeremiah 32:27; Job 38:4; Exodus 15:11)
- in all places (Proverbs 15:3; Psalm 139:7-13; Psalm 135:6)
- and at all times (Psalm 93:2; Exodus 15:18; Revelation 22:13),

there is no need for other gods.

No wonder He does not tolerate their worship (Exodus 20:3; Deuteronomy 4:23; Acts 15:20); for that sends the message that His power is insufficient and that reinforcements are needed.

But that is not the case.

OUR GOD IS ONE GOD.

PRAISE HIS NAME.

13

Our Source for Help

When the people of God make alliances with the enemy and depend on him for assistance, it never ends well. Though at first, it may seem to work just fine, it puts a stain on our spiritual character and pushes us away from God.

King Asa of Judah called on his ally, King Benhadad of Syria, to rescue him from the King of Israel. Payment was offered in the form of all the silver and gold in the Lord's temple and in the King's house (1 Kings 15:18).

We cannot take what belongs to God and give it to the enemy. Whether it is our money, our time, our talents and gifts, they belong to God.

Asa was saved by the King of Syria. However, this refusal by King Asa to acknowledge that God was the One from whom help should be sought, brought the judgement of God upon him (2 Chronicles 16:7-12).

Though he had previously trusted God in a seemingly hopeless situation (2 Chronicles 14:9 -15), he grew stubborn and rebellious after this act.

His relationship with the Lord deteriorated further. He imprisoned the prophet of God who tried to correct him, oppressed the people, and was struck with a disease in his feet. He never sought the help of God and died in that state.

We, the people of God, must remember from where our help comes (Psalm 121:2).

14

Anointed for a Purpose

We need the anointing of God on our lives as we seek to engage the enemy in battle. The anointing enabled David to defeat Goliath (1 Samuel 16:13; 17:49). The anointing upon Samson made him physically strong as he fought the Philistines (Judges 15:14; 16:3).

However, his constant foolish acts and resulting web of lies caused the anointing to depart without his knowledge (Judges 16:20). He was easily captured and bound, his eyes were put out, and he was made to serve the enemy, providing entertainment as well (Judges 16:21-25).

When the anointing departs, it is always sad and it puts into play a sequence of events, all unpleasant. Samson lost his vision. When you lose your vision, you easily fall into traps, can be led down the wrong path, and can no longer identify important differences. Spiritual vision is very important.

You can be made to serve in the camp of the enemy, can be put up on display, and be forced to provide amusement in that camp. Embarrassment, humiliation, and complete lack of self-will are signs of capture by the enemy. As a flood, the enemy comes in (Isaiah 59:19) but there is no help, for the anointing is gone. Now the enemy has his way.

Do not take the anointing for granted. It is to be used to help build the Kingdom of God, not for personal gain (money or fame), not for entertainment, and not to impress others. Samson made that error (Judges 14:5-19; 16:1-3) and lost it all.

The anointing comes with a specific purpose (Isaiah 61:1-3).

Let us fulfil the purpose of God in our lives.

15

Food

Food is one of the essentials of life. While on earth, our Lord Himself experienced the pangs of hunger (Mark 11:12). He understands what it feels like to survey empty cupboards and empty refrigerators, but He provides.

The birds do not cultivate crops nor tend livestock, yet they eat. If He provides for birds, what about us? (Matthew 6:26). Not only does He provide for birds, but He also provides for other wildlife (Psalm 104:21).

Out of the ground, the Lord formed every beast, every bird, and man, but into man He breathed the breath of life (Genesis 2:7,19). So since He provides for them, He will also provide for us.

Jesus performed miracles involving food. He fed thousands starting off with just enough for one person (Matthew 14:19; 15:36). Jesus even prepared breakfast for His disciples on the beach after His resurrection (John 21:9).

The Lord used ravens to bring food to the prophet Elijah during a drought (1 Kings 17:6). Then He commanded a struggling widow to feed him. A handful of meal fed the prophet, the widow, and her son for a year (1 Kings 17:12-16).

The prophet Elisha fed 100 men with food that was not nearly enough (2 Kings 4:43).

If what you have is not enough to meet your needs, TRUST HIM.

GOD PROVIDES.

GOD MULTIPLIES.

He knows what we need (Matthew 6:32) and He loves us.

16

Naaman

2 Kings 5

Naaman appeared to have it all. He had a great job, performed well, and was liked and appreciated by his boss. He was brave and of sound character. His reputation was well established.

However, he had a problem: leprosy; an incurable and eventually disfiguring disease. God used a little maid in his household to get him to Samaria in contact with the prophet Elisha.

Naaman had quite a trip. The whole thing started when the maid spoke to her mistress, Naaman's wife. Naaman promptly went to the king, his boss. He was sent from one king to another, then sent to the prophet's house where a messenger told him to go dip in the Jordan River seven times.

Naaman was outraged at the fact that the prophet did not see it fit to speak to him and pray for him in person, sending a messenger. Then, the message upset him further. He was not a man to annoy. He had a powerful position, however again, God used an underling to speak to him. He agreed to go to the Jordan River and dip.

He had not been given a test of endurance, a test of strength, a test of character, a test of bravery, or a test of patriotism. His was a simple test, one of obedience and faith. He complied, received his miracle of healing, and was converted. He recognised who was the true God and purposed in his heart to worship no other. That is a sign of true conversion.

God may be testing our obedience and our faith. Getting annoyed at the messenger and the message will bring us no profit. God can use the unexpected and the unusual. Have faith and obey.

17

Race

Racism is not just a current problem. It has been a problem for thousands of years (Numbers 12:1).

However, we must understand that we were created in His image (Genesis 1:26), and we are all equal in His sight.

Facts of history, geography, economics, and religion have led some to believe that they are superior and have more rights than others. But God never intended it to be so.

Imagine if the entire earth belonged to one race, though, in a way it does. I speak of the human race. But suppose we all looked the same—in skin colour, eyes, hair texture—sounds boring, doesn't it?

Look around at nature; are all birds the same? Do all plants look alike?

God made us all of one blood (Acts 17:26).

Let us appreciate the diversity.

18

Preparation

He prepares a table for us (Psalm 23:5). We are not being fed leftovers, scraps, or items from a doggie bag!

He is preparing for us.

He is also preparing mansions for us (John 14:2).

But we are not without responsibility.

We have to prepare to meet Him (Amos 4:12).

Let us not be unprepared as the wedding guest (Matthew 22:11).

For, like him, we will have no excuse.

Are we prepared? (Matthew 24:44)

19

Legacy

King Jeroboam of Israel was insecure in his position. He allowed himself to be overcome with fear and apprehension and that led him to idolatry. The entire nation followed his lead from that time on (2 Kings 17:22).

He sinned in building two golden calves and erecting them in Bethel and Dan so that the Israelites would not need to go to Jerusalem to worship and thereby go back on their loyalty to him (1 Kings 12:26-30).

Upon examination, his motive and his fear seem reasonable in terms of human logic. However, he forgot three important things.

1. God had chosen Jerusalem to put His Name there (2 Chronicles 6:6).
2. God did not allow idolatry (Exodus 20:4-5).
3. God had given him the throne (1 Kings 14:7).

His sin affected him and his generation, and the entire nation was cursed (1 Kings 14:10-16). Generations of succeeding kings stumbled because of his sin (1 Kings 16; 2 Kings 13:2) and were compared to Jeroboam.

The nation continued to be tied down by curses associated with his sin (2 Kings 10:32) until they lost their nationhood (2 Kings 17:22-23).

It was not the first time the children of Israel, as a nation, had worshipped a golden calf. In the wilderness, shortly after leaving Egypt, was the first time (Exodus 32:2-4); punishment followed (Exodus 32:35). This time, there were two golden calves built by Jeroboam, newly returned from Egypt himself (1 Kings 12:2).

Seems as if it was easier for them to leave Egypt than for Egypt to leave them.

When we come out of the world spiritually or accept Christ as our Saviour, old habits may try to overcome us. We need to surrender completely to the Lord.

Let us examine the type of legacy we are leaving behind. With what will our names be associated after our departure?

The name of Jeroboam is associated with unbelief, idolatry, rebellion, disobedience, ungodly leadership, and cursed generations.

True, we are not ruling a nation, but we all have influence on someone's life.

Let us follow God completely to ensure that our legacy is one of righteousness.

20

Altars

The Old Testament tabernacle and its court could be divided into three broad zones. The first, near the entrance, was dominated by the altar of sacrifice. This was a brasen altar where animal sacrifices were offered for sin. This area was accessible to all (Exodus 40:6).

The altar of incense was found in the tabernacle itself, in the second zone. This altar was covered with gold. Here, priests burnt sweet incense daily. Unauthorised persons were not allowed to make or even possess this incense. Only priests were allowed here (Exodus 30).

In the third zone, deeper inside, was the ark of the covenant where the presence of God dwelt. Only the high priest could enter this zone and that was once a year (Leviticus 16).

Getting to His presence was a process. In today's world, persons are desirous of entering the presence of God but are unwilling to first go to the altar of sacrifice. For doing so would amount to an admission of a sinful nature and the need for a Saviour.

The altar of sacrifice was a place of hard work. No halfway measures could be made here. Blood was shed and a life was lost.

Christ freely offered Himself for our sins, and once we accept His sacrifice, we are made priests (Revelation 1:5-6). This gives us access to the sweet presence of God.

Various means as thinking positive and happy thoughts,

meditating, practicing yoga, reciting different chants, performing various rites, and doing charitable work are being tried to attain that place in our world today.

But there is only ONE way—that is through the blood of the sinless lamb, JESUS. There are no short cuts, no alternate routes. These are deceptive and dangerous. They lead elsewhere, not to God.

21

Speak Right

We get upset when people say things about us that are not true.

Those hurt feelings and anger may be justified. Who wants to be lied upon and misrepresented?

God is also not pleased when people say things about Him that are not true (Job 42:7).

The acquaintances of Job had spoken quite a lot over an extended period.

That did not mean that their words were not heard by the Lord. The fact that He had said nothing at the time did not mean He intended to ignore them and their words.

We must be careful, when we speak about Him, to say the correct thing.

Speak His Word. We are on stable ground there.

His Word shall stand forever (Isaiah 40:8).

His Word shall not return to Him unaccomplished (Isaiah 55:11).

He magnifies His Word above His Name (Psalm 138:2).

22

Glory Belongs to Him

2 Kings 19

The King of Assyria, a mighty king by the standards of men, allowed his battlefield successes to go to his head. Indeed, he and his father had conquered many nations, so his pride seemed justified.

But he made three fatal errors:

- He never realised that the victories won were not due to skill and power, but rather, was the will of God.

- He compared the God of Israel to the gods of the conquered nations. After all, they had been unable to deliver their people and had been thrown into the fire.

- He assumed that Jerusalem was just another city to be conquered. He had no way of knowing that Jerusalem was special to God (2 Chronicles 6:6).

He openly boasted that God could not deliver Jerusalem and King Hezekiah. He thought everything was under his control.

But God was listening. Things went very badly for him and his army. Death and defeat were their end. It turned out that his god was unable to save him.

We sometimes think that our own successes are due to our skill, hard work, good luck, or even our consultations with those who claim to have supernatural abilities.

The will of God supersedes all the above (Isaiah 46:10). King Herod also believed in his own power and met a sorry end (Acts 12:23).

All the glory belongs to God, the true God (Isaiah 42:8; 1 Corinthians 1:29).

23

The Love of God

Romans 8:38, 39

The love of God is:
- Deep
- Rich
- Undeserved
- Fathomless

He took no halfway measures (John 3:16).

If He had, where would we be?

Why are we trying to take halfway measures with Him?

24

Light and Sound

Light and sound travel at great speeds but light travels faster and over further distances than sound. The sun is millions of miles away from earth, but its light reaches us.

Sound, on the other hand, has a range over which it can be heard. On some days, we can see distant lightning but not hear the thunder. When it is closer to us, we see the lightning flash before we hear the roar of the thunder. This is because light travels faster than sound.

Light penetrates darkness. It is never too dark for light to be seen. Darkness cannot obstruct light. Light makes a difference. Life on earth would be impossible without light.

Jesus is the light of the world and so are we (John 8:12; Matthew 5:14). Much darkness, evil, and sin exist in the world (John 3:19, 20). But we must let our light shine (Matthew 5:16) and not just complain about the darkness.

The light shining in us travels faster and over greater distances than what we say, for that has a limited range. Only those close to us will hear our words but those further away can see our actions and be impacted by them.

Keep shining even if you are not understood (John 1:5). Shine on for Jesus.

25

Siege

"Now Jericho was straitly shut up because of the children of Israel: none went out, and none came in." (Joshua 6:1)

We are supposed to make the enemy uncomfortable, cause inconvenience and uncertainty, and bring some level of departure from the norm.

But it is frequently the other way around.

We, the people of God, should not be constantly living in fear of attack. Yes, there are times when we are attacked, times when we have to stand still while the Lord fights for us (Exodus 14:13-14), and there are times when we are called to the battle (Numbers 31:6).

It should not be the case where the enemy has us surrounded permanently and we are under siege, backed into a corner.

We may think the enemy is too strong for us (Numbers 13:31), and he is, if we go against him in our strength (Numbers 14:42).

Let us take our rightful place in the Lord. Live in victory, in spite of the battles that come our way from time to time. For the battles are not ours but His (2 Chronicles 20:15).

26

Clear the Channel

The children of Israel suffered defeat on the battlefield whenever there was sin in their lives or in the camp (Numbers 14:40-45; Joshua 7).

Now that is a good reason to keep the channel between us and the Lord clear of sin. Another good reason is found in Psalm 66:18 and Isaiah 59:2. No one wants their prayers to God to remain unanswered.

Another powerful reason is that sin will keep us out of Heaven, and since there is only one other alternative to which no one wants to go, especially a 'believer' (Revelation 21:8), why not aim to keep the channel clear?

Some sins are obvious, and we tend to focus on them. They are sexual sins, lying, swearing, and stealing. However, the more subtle ones include:

- Envy (Exodus 20:17)
- Lack of love towards the brethren (1 John 2:11)
- Anger and bitterness (Ephesians 4:31)
- Racism (Numbers 12:1-10)
- Rebellion and disobedience (1 Samuel 15:23)

These are often overlooked. We sometimes fail to remember that sin is sin.

Let us keep those channels clear by asking God to search us (Psalm 139:23-24), by forgiving others and asking His forgiveness (Luke 6:37; 1 John 1:9), and by praying for each other (Job 42:10; James 5:16).

Defeat in battle, unanswered prayers, and ultimately, eternal separation from God are consequences of sin in our lives.

CLEAR THE CHANNEL!

27

Substitute

In his lifetime, King David made great preparations to build the house of God. He dedicated vessels unto the Lord (2 Samuel 8:10-11).

When his son, Solomon, built the temple, he gathered the vessels his father had dedicated and put them together with the ones he himself had made (1 Kings 7:48-51).

Apart from the temple, Solomon also built his own house, the house of the forest of Lebanon (1 Kings 7:1-2), a house for the daughter of Pharaoh, and other projects.

Gold was used freely (1 Kings 10:21). It was an era of great wealth, but it would not last. Solomon allied himself with Pharaoh, married his daughter and many other women of the nations against whom God had spoken (Exodus 34:14-16; 1 Kings 11:1-2).

After the death of Solomon, the reigning king of Egypt attacked Jerusalem. The son of Solomon was powerless against him. The Egyptians carried away all the precious vessels of the temple and of the king's house (1 Kings 14:25, 26).

The impressive shields of gold which Solomon had made, all 300 of them, each made of three pounds of gold, were also carried off (1 Kings 10:17).

What was the response?

Solomon's son did not try to retrieve them, for he knew he was no match for the enemy. Instead, he replaced them with shields of brass, a material to which little attention was paid during the reign of his father (1 Kings 7:47). What we have is really a cheap substitute, easily discernable by a knowledgeable onlooker, and though the replacement shields were closely guarded (1 Kings 14:27), that did not increase their value.

The actions of one generation of believers affect the spiritual well-being of future generations. When we compromise and fail to serve God wholeheartedly (Numbers 14:24), we endanger not only ourselves but also those of the future. We are weakened, and it becomes very easy for the enemy to rob us of what is genuine and precious in the house of God and in our lives.

Rather than try to get it back, we replace it with cheap substitutes. The enemy has no interest in imitations or what has no value. He goes straight for the valuable and genuine.

If we compare the sight of 300 shields of pure gold to that of brass, the latter falls short exceedingly.

So too, does whatever substitute we come up with to fill the void left after we have allowed the enemy to take away the valuable. It was not just our spiritual labour but rather the combined efforts of our forefathers in the faith that left us those precious shields.

They are easily lost to the enemy and, in our weakened state, cannot be retrieved.

We should remain strong in the Lord (Ephesians 6:10), continue to move forward in Him, and give no place to the enemy (Ephesians 4:27).

We should make no affinity with Pharaoh, keep our worship pure, and serve God wholeheartedly. Do not allow the enemy to cause us to lose our most precious assets in the Lord.

28

Be Ready

"Therefore be ye also ready: for in such an hour as ye think not the Son of man cometh." Matthew 24:44

When we are not expecting Him, He will put in His appearance. Just as a thief strikes, so will be the coming of our Lord (1 Thessalonians 5:2). It is not that we are to be in an agitated state or constantly wish His return so we could escape our debts, our relatives, our neighbours, or our bosses. It is intended that in all we think, say, and do, the thought should be in our minds: **"I HAVE TO BE READY."**.

How many hasty words, ill-advised actions, and secret thoughts would never occur? Without these, we would have avoided many issues, conflicts, separations, and divorces.

If every Christian lived their lives bearing the soon return of our Lord in mind, our homes, communities, churches, and nations would be different.

There must also be a healthy balance. Christ never intended for us to sit back, relax and await His return (Luke 19:13). Some have made that error and lived to regret it. They failed to prepare for examinations, failed to invest, failed to save, and failed to start families.

There are others who trusted in the words of some individual who gave a date for His return.

The Bible tells us that no one knows the date of His return; no human being, even no angel (Matthew 24:36).

Our eternal life is so important that the present life with its challenges, issues, storms, fears, or even its accomplishments, fades away in comparison (Romans 8:18).

LET US BE WISE.

LET US LIVE OUR LIVES IN THE LORD, TO ITS FULLEST.

LET US BE READY.

29

The Crowd

Even if everybody else is doing it, that is no reason for you to go along with the crowd if a violation of the law of God is involved.

For one, it may just seem like everyone is doing it, but the Lord may have a true remnant left (1 Kings 19:18), and even if it is true that no one else is following Him, you should stand your ground (Daniel 3:18).

Adam, Noah, and Lot were the only men who could truly be sure what everyone else was or was not doing.

God will hold you responsible for your own actions, not the actions of others.

Remember that the next time you are tempted to go along with the crowd on the wrong road (Matthew 7:13-14).

30

Universal Praise

Psalm 148

The praises start high up in the heavens.

The heavenly host join in.

WHY?

He spoke them into being, not just temporarily, but forever.

From the earth, the praises ring out from deep down—fearsome creatures and elements of the weather which also move at His command are included.

Landforms, fruit-bearing trees, timber-producing trees, wildlife, domesticated animals, birds, and things that crawl, all praise Him.

Then the people join in—rulers, judges and the people they lead, people of both genders and of all ages—**PRAISE HIM!!**

PRAISE HIM FOR HIS NAME!

PRAISE HIM FOR HIS GLORY!

PRAISE HIM FOR HIS MAJESTY!

PRAISE HIM FOR HIS TENDER LOVE!

EVERYONE HAS A REASON TO PRAISE.
OH, PRAISE HIM!!!

31

Final

"And I saw the dead, small and great, stand before God; and the books were opened: and another book was opened, which is the book of life: and the dead were judged out of those things which were written in the books, according to their works." Revelation 20:12.

The revelation of things to come could be scary and troubling but these writings are for our benefit.

Death is not the end. It simply ushers us into a new phase—an eternal or never-ending one.

What happens to us after death depends entirely on our actions in our lifetime. Did we believe in Jesus or not? (Acts 16:31)

The dead will not be judged according to their social status, their wealth, or their poverty, or even their religion.

They will not be judged according to their race, ethnicity, or nationality.

The dead will be judged according to the records in Heaven.

"For the LORD is our judge…" (Isaiah 33:22)

AND HIS DECISION IS FINAL.

32

Camera

In our high-tech world, many persons have installed security cameras around their homes and business places. These cameras monitor movements in and around their properties.

Some are so advanced that they constantly rotate to get an all-around view. Others detect movement in their vicinity and turn to follow the activity.

We hope these cameras also serve as a deterrent to the criminal element. Over the years, criminals have come up with means to avoid, sabotage and even destroy cameras.

Isn't it comforting to know that the eyes of our Lord cannot be escaped, cannot be sabotaged, and do not sleep?

- 2 Chronicles 16:9
- Proverbs 15:3
- Psalm 34:15
- Psalm 121:4

33

Hedge

Years ago, one of our neighbours kept a beautiful hedge at the front of his property. He maintained it carefully, a thick, tall bushy barrier. It prevented prying eyes, gave a sense of beauty, and offered protection.

One day a vehicle ran off the road straight into his hedge. It never got any further. The hedge had done its job.

God has a hedge around us. The devil bitterly complained to God about the hedge around Job (Job 1:10). You see, the devil had been trying to get to Job, his family, and his business, but the hedge was sturdy.

He has been trying to get to us, too, but the hedge is holding. We never see most of the attacks from the enemy and never feel their effects. If we did, life would be a lot more difficult, believe it or not.

We thank You Father for Your divine protection.

34

Sent by God

Genesis 37 gives the account of Joseph, a young son who is very close to his father and has envious brothers who sell him into slavery.

One day, Joseph is his father's favourite son; the next, he is a slave in a foreign land. Quite a change for a teenager.

Nowhere in the Genesis account of his being sold into slavery does it tell us of the involvement of God. We see only a favourite son, a doting father, and mean, envious brothers. Joseph is off the scene.

His father, who is led to believe he is dead, is inconsolable and plans to continue grieving for him for the rest of his life. However, it was all in the plan of God.

"He sent a man before them, even Joseph, who was sold for a servant:" (Psalm 105:17)

Joseph had been sent to Egypt by God to make provision for not only His people but for others as well (Genesis 41:57).

Yet, he was sent as a slave. He was not sent as a wealthy merchant, an intellectual, or even as an adult. He looked helpless and vulnerable, just as a baby lying in a manger (Luke 2:7).

It did not look as if Joseph was being sent by God. Joseph certainly did not feel that he was on a mission from God. His brothers did not think they were a part of God's plan and their father had no idea that God was involved.

Frequently, we do not see the involvement of God in our lives and it looks as though things are just happening to us and around us.

Joseph had been given glimpses of his destiny in his dreams. Maybe, we too have been given glimpses in our dreams.

Some of the involvement of God in our lives is evident right away; others become obvious as the years roll by, and there are others that we will never recognise in this life. Whichever way it happens, know that His hand is in our lives.

35

Just Imagine

If God shared all His plans for us (Jeremiah 29:11) and when and why He intended to carry them out; then we would:

- Accuse Him of acting unfairly
- Critique the plan
- Desire the inclusion or exclusion of some individuals
- Invite other contributions
- Lodge appeals
- Offer our own plan
- Request changes in the timeframe
- Seek other opinions
- Suggest alternatives
- Voice objections

Still wondering why He acts the way He does?

36

One Touch

God is so powerful that all we need from Him is one touch.

Jesus touched the coffin of a widow's son in Nain (Luke 7:14-15). She and her son are not even named in the Bible, but one touch changed their lives.

Jacob never forgot the night he struggled with the angel. One touch affected him physically for the rest of his life, but more importantly, he received the blessings he sought (Genesis 32:25).

Daniel (Daniel 10:10), Elijah (1 Kings 19:5-8), and the Apostle John (Revelation 1:17), all benefitted from one touch, and so can we.

Elijah, however, had a second touch, for he had a 40-day fasting journey ahead, while he continued to flee from the enemy, on foot.

The woman with the issue of blood (Matthew 9:21) took the initiative.

We do not have to be passive; Jacob was not, neither was Daniel. Let us actively seek Him and His touch. Our lives will never be the same.

May we desire a touch from Him, for in that, there is the protection we seek in this dangerous time, the stability we crave in this time of change, and the assurance we need in the midst of fear.

TOUCH US, O MASTER!

37

Fight

1 Kings 20

King Ahab, more known for his evil ways, provides an example of the delivering power of God. The king of Syria made a claim on all that belonged to Ahab. He claimed his gold, his silver, his wives, and his children. Ahab offered no resistance.

When the enemy realised that Ahab was not going to put up a fight, he gave him one day's notice that he would be sending his servants to tour the king's house and the houses of his employees. They would be free to take away whatever they desired. That was too much. Those close to King Ahab advised resistance.

It was at this point that God intervened. He sent a prophet with a word for Ahab. An extraordinary victory on the battlefield resulted.

1 Samuel 11

The people of Jabesh Gilead also offered no resistance as Nahash the Ammonite came up and besieged them. They agreed to serve him without putting up a fight.

However, the enemy wanted more. Nahash the Ammonite would accept their surrender only if they gave up their right eyes, *literally*. He intended to first put out all their right eyes before they served him.

God used King Saul to bring deliverance to them, but the deliverance only came after they made some effort to seek help.

RESIST THE DEVIL (James 4:7)

Don't be a pushover for the enemy. He is never satisfied.

Do not roll over and allow the enemy to encroach more and more into your territory.

If he gets our health easily, he wants our finances. If he gets our marriage, he wants our children.

Fight!!

Victory is ours.

King Ahab would have missed out on an amazing victory on the battlefield. The people of Jabesh Gilead would have lived the rest of their lives as slaves with distorted vision.

What have we given up?

We, the people of God, need to engage in spiritual battle rather than give up in fear and in despair.

PRAY, FAST, READ AND STUDY HIS WORD,

LIVE HOLY, TRUST HIM, OBEY HIM.

38

This Time Tomorrow

2 Kings 7

The situation in Samaria was desperate. A famine caused by a siege mounted by the King of Syria had brought people to cannibalism (2 Kings 6:28). They had reached their lowest point.

Elisha brought a Word from the Lord. Things were about to change drastically in the space of 24 hours. Good food would be abundant and sold at a reasonable price in a short space of time.

The King's right-hand man openly doubted. He voiced his scepticism that not even God could do that. Immediate judgement was pronounced on him. He would see it but not benefit from it.

The Word of God proved true while the words of this official were shown to be a lie (Numbers 23:19). The Word of God is powerful (Hebrews 4:12). His Word was in creation. His Word became flesh and dwelt among us (John 1:1,14). By His Word, He performed many miracles (Psalm 107:20; Matthew 8:16; Mark 4:39). He does not appreciate persons doubting or challenging His Word. Doubting God's Word is doubting God.

The children of Israel reasoned: *Well, yes, God did some powerful things in the past, but can He handle this situation?* (Psalm 78:12-31). The judgement of God came upon them.

God can change your situation quickly or gradually, or

He can change you to better handle it. Read His Word. Believe His Word. Obey His Word. God is in control.

39

Goodness of God

"...the goodness of God leadeth thee to repentance" (Romans 2:4)

God has been good to us. Yes, we all have issues, but they do not take away from the fact that He has been good.

His goodness should make us want to repent and turn our lives to Him. Think of all He has done. We will be amazed at the number of blessings that have come our way.

Blessings unrecognised, blessings unappreciated, and blessings taken for granted. Every day, find something to thank Him for, and praise Him throughout the day for that thing. Soon you will develop a grateful attitude that will spill over into the rest of your life.

Acknowledge His presence in your life. Repent of your wrongdoings and sins, and purpose in your heart to serve Him and love Him for the rest of your life.

40

Harvest

"Be not deceived; God is not mocked: for whatsoever a man soweth, that shall he also reap." Galatians 6:7

This is a law that applies to the realm of the natural and of the spiritual. Those who invest in the flesh or put all their efforts, time, money, and energy into things that do not last, shall be rewarded with similar things. These will bring some pleasure for a short while before they vanish.

Those who invest in the Spirit, that is, expend effort, time, money, and energy in spiritual matters shall reap spiritual benefits.

We sometimes look at persons who have a great anointing on their lives and wish it upon ourselves, but are we willing to sow what they did?

This rule applies to the agricultural sector as well. It is useless viewing a farmer's field and wishing we had a similar harvest. The fact is that we did not sow what he did and in the amounts that he did. Also, no farmer who sowed a field of pigeon peas reaps a field of tomatoes instead. However, this principle means more than wicked people who commit acts of wickedness and cruelty will have the same done to them in this life and the next; and those who are kind-hearted will reap kind deeds.

This is true but we can be easily fooled by pretenders; however, God is never fooled, never deceived, for He sees beyond what we see (1 Samuel 16:7) and knows exactly what is being sown.

He is not taken in by outward pretentious displays performed by evil hearts.

Let us sow in the Spirit, liberally. Prayer, fasting, and the study of His Word are spiritual seeds to be sown in great abundance.

Our harvest will be great and extend into the eternal.

41

Different Paths

God chooses different paths for us all. We often wonder why. One day it will become clear, though for now, we may be puzzled.

The prophet Elijah was taken up into Heaven by a chariot of fire (2 Kings 2:11), while his successor Elisha got sick and died (2 Kings 13:14).

Strangely, the anointing remained on him even after his burial (2 Kings 13:21).

The apostle James was imprisoned and executed (Acts 12:2). Peter, whom it was intended should suffer the same fate soon after, was freed by an angel (Acts 12:7). History records that John died of natural causes after attempts to kill him had failed.

Our sovereign God orders our steps (Psalm 37:23) and our lives (Psalm 37:18). Stressing out about tomorrow brings no benefits and is ill-advised (Matthew 6:34).

God knows the end from the beginning (Isaiah 46:10). He is never surprised, never left in a panic, never caught off-guard, never left wringing His hands, and never in a state of shock.

We need to keep reminding ourselves that God is not a man (Numbers 23:19). If He were, it would mean that another human being was ordering our lives. That thought could be pretty discomforting.

BUT, GOD IS IN CONTROL.

42

Make Room

2 Kings 4:8-37

As the prophet Elisha went about the country, he encountered a woman who often invited him to eat at her home. She was not a poor woman. Her husband was older and owned agricultural fields.

One day she realised that the man of God needed more than an invitation to dinner. He needed a place to stay whenever he was in the area. She consulted her husband and built a loft, furnishing it nicely, to the standards of the day.

The prophet had not asked her to do it. God had not commanded her, as He did in 1 Kings 17:9, but she saw a need, knew she had the necessary resources, and did something about it. She carved out a space from what was available to her. A loft is made using space that already exists.

We too need to carve out a space, a dedicated space for the Lord, for the study of His Word, for prayer, and for fasting. The space is already there. So is the time. It needs to be appropriately used.

If we see a need and know we can help, we should. We should not say that we are already contributing. This woman was already feeding the prophet, but she saw the need to do more.

She did extra and received extra blessings. She went from being childless to being the mother of a son. When he fell ill and died, he was restored to life in the same space she had carved out.

You can receive spiritual gifts in that space that you dedicated to the LORD.

She was warned about a coming famine, told of its length, and advised to migrate. After the famine, she returned and benefitted from the full restoration of all her property and its earnings (2 Kings 8:1-6).

An unexpected son, resurrected life, spared difficulty, and complete restoration were all hers because she saw a need and did something about it.

We too can be shielded from stressful situations because we make space for Him.

God can provide relief from some other source if we refuse to help (Esther 4:14), but we would be cheating ourselves of unimagined blessings.

43

It Seems Right

"There is a way which seemeth right unto a man, but the end thereof are the ways of death" (Proverbs 14:12)

It seems right, but it isn't. By the time we discover it is not right, it may be too late.

If it seemed wrong, fewer persons would follow it. Things are not always as they seem. Life can be tricky. Sometimes we get confused in the grey areas.

CHRIST IS THE WAY, THE TRUTH AND THE LIFE (John 14:6).

No grey area here.

FOLLOW HIM. HE IS THE WAY.

44

Declaration

"The heavens declare the glory of God..." (Psalm 19:1)

What a declaration!

They speak loudly everywhere. No one can claim not to hear them.

They are His handiwork, and they speak volumes.

There they are for all to see, displaying splendour and beauty that gives us an insight into the ONE who made them.

They are extensive, without number, and without borders.

No one doubts their existence, their reliability. Why doubt the GOD who made them?

When seeking employment, we prepare resumes that list our qualifications and achievements.

Well, what is listed on the resume of other gods?

Look at what our God can do.

"...stretcheth out the heavens as a curtain, and spreadeth them out as a tent to dwell in" (Isaiah 40:22)

Oh Yes! He is that great.

Think of what He can do in our lives.

45

On Your Side

How many times have we been told the following?

- *"I wish I could help, but this is a bad time for me."*
- *"Maybe if your group contained more persons, I would be able to help."*
- *"Your earnings are not enough. There is no way that can happen."*
- *"Maybe if you were 10, 20 years younger…"*

We human beings and our institutions have many limitations. What a relief that they do not extend to God.

2 Chronicles 14:11

Your circumstances do not determine the outcome of your situation. Once God is in the equation, the result can be surprising.

1 Samuel 14:6

God is not restricted by numbers. He never needs backup or reinforcements.

You are His child, living for Him and serving Him.

You are not outnumbered nor underprivileged.

The MIGHTY GOD is on your side.

46

In Joseph's Position

Genesis 37, 39-45

Favourite son

My daddy loves me, and my brothers are envious. I report their mischief.

Slave

I did not think my brothers would sink so low to sell me to foreigners. My father loves me. You can't treat me like this.

Supervisor

Things are better but I am still a slave in a foreign land. My master is away a lot and his wife has been looking at me strangely. Lord, keep her away from me.

Prisoner

Lord, really! My master's wife should be the one in prison, not me. Is this what I get for being faithful to You?

Prisoner-in-charge

Some improvement, but I am still in prison. You have given me these gifts of dream interpretation and caring leadership, but how am I supposed to use them here? I want my freedom.

President

Lord... Thank you for freedom, promotion and a spirit of forgiveness. Thank You for giving me a wife, and healing and restoration in my family. Thank You for making me a blessing.

47

Enemies

Want to see your enemies calm down?
Let your ways please Him (Proverbs 16:7).
In other words:
- No wishing evil upon them
- No rejoicing when they fall
- No broadcasting of their evil deeds
- No anticipating their descent into hell

We would consider those who crucified our Lord to be enemies.

"...Father, forgive them; for they know not what they do..." (Luke 23:34)

Those who stoned an innocent believer to death are surely his enemies.

"...Lord, lay not this sin to their charge..." (Acts 7:60).

Pray for your enemies (Matthew 5:44).

They really need it and so do you.

And if your enemies fall into the category of Alexander the coppersmith (2 Timothy 4:14), the Lord is quite capable of handling them without your input.

48

Response

How we respond to the Word of God is very important.

King Josiah was repentant when the Word of God was read to him. Evil had been pronounced against his land.

- His heart was tender.
- He humbled himself.
- He rent his clothes.
- He wept

(2 Kings 22:19)

Even Ahab, with a well-earned reputation for being the most wicked king, repented when he heard God's Word (1 Kings 21:27).

Compare these responses to that of King Jehoiakim, who was so annoyed when he heard the Word of the Lord that he threw the written roll into the fire (Jeremiah 36:21-25).

We have the written Word of God. How do we respond when we read it or when we hear His spoken Word delivered by his servants?

For apart from seeing our outward actions, He also sees our deepest thoughts (Hebrews 4:12).

49

Knowledge

In Egypt, in the days of Joseph, the magicians and so-called wise men could not interpret Pharaoh's dream.

Only the servant of God could (Genesis 41:15).

In Babylon, in the days of Belshazzar, the astrologers and soothsayers could not interpret the writing on the wall.

Only the servant of God could (Daniel 5:12).

Daniel had also been the only one who could interpret the dreams of Nebuchadnezzar (Daniel 2:25; 4:7-8).

In these days of numerous palm readers, fortune tellers, and others who claim to have all power and all knowledge, let us remember that it is in God that all knowledge dwells (Colossians 2:3).

50

Dwelling Place

The magnificent temple built by King Solomon could not contain God, neither can heaven and the heaven of heavens (2 Chronicles 6:18).

Yet He chooses to dwell in us (1 Corinthians 3:16). This is a wonderful privilege not to be taken lightly.

May we not forget Who dwells in us, for He does not dwell in temples made by hands (Acts 7:48).

Bless His Holy Name!

51

The Lord Himself

It is a common practice among senior politicians to have other persons represent them at functions and meetings. It would be quite impossible for them to personally attend each event.

At the coming of our Lord, no heaven-sent representative will take His place.

1 Thessalonians 4:16-17

"For the Lord himself shall descend from heaven with a shout, with the voice of the archangel, and with the trump of God: and the dead in Christ shall rise first:

Then we which are alive and remain shall be caught up together with them in the clouds, to meet the Lord in the air: and so shall we ever be with the Lord."

This is our hope. This is what we eagerly await. Whether we are numbered with the dead in Christ or with those who are alive and remain is not important, for we shall all be with Him.

When we consider this, everyday stresses and disappointments do not seem so overwhelming anymore.

Like the small child on Christmas morning disregarding the bruise on his knee as he views unopened presents, let our anticipation to meet Him overshadow our struggles.

"Even so, come, Lord Jesus" (Revelation 22:20).

52

Don't Compound It

When David sinned by committing adultery with Bathsheba, he compounded the issue by murdering her husband (2 Samuel 11).

When the children of Judah fled into Egypt to escape the punishment of God, they compounded the matter by refusing to listen to His Word and by worshipping other gods there. They were bold and vocal in their sin, but the hand of God reached them in their hideout (Jeremiah 44).

The children of Judah, who were in exile under the King of Persia, knew why their beloved city of Jerusalem had been overrun. That was a consequence of their sin. It was not a surprise. Rather than repenting of their sin in the strange land to which they had been carried, they went on to break even more of the law of God by having strange wives and children by them (Ezra 10).

Sin tends to multiply and produce situations that become more and more difficult to contain. Even the priests who had specific instructions about whom they should marry (Leviticus 21:7) had fallen into this trap.

When we sin, we should repent immediately, not compound it by sinning further to cover the initial sin or to display further rebellion.

There were consequences for David, though he eventually repented, and there would have been unpleasant consequences for those married to strange wives.

Keep it simple, repent immediately.

53

Steps to Victory

Consult the One-in-charge regularly: (1 Chronicles 14:14). That way, you will be aware of changes in strategy. Pray constantly (Luke 18:1).

Be appropriately attired: No one goes into battle in their night clothes or in dinner party attire. Complete armour is required (Ephesians 6:11). Any area left exposed will be targeted by the enemy.

Prior training: Soldiers must be trained. Men snatched from off the street and sent into battle cause disaster. Prayer, fasting, and the study of His Word are all battle training.

Identify the real enemy: You must know who the enemy is. Your neighbour, boss, sibling, or spouse may look like the enemy, but our adversary is the devil (1 Peter 5:8).

Have a battle plan: Don't rush out onto the battlefield not knowing how to respond to the possibilities (1 Chronicles 19:10-14, Nehemiah 4:20).

Stay alert: Distraction on the battlefield can be dangerous to you and those around you (1 Peter 5:8).

Call for help: Do not see yourself going down and continue in the same fashion. This is not a one-man show (1 Chronicles 19:12, James 5:14).

Look out for spies, traitors, the fearful and unwilling: Do not assume we all have the same goal. Some persons have different agendas and will hinder your progress

(Matthew 13:25; Judges 7:3) Stay close to like-minded individuals.

In conclusion: May we all be able to speak like the apostle Paul (2 Timothy 4:7).

54

Influence

The new coronavirus is wreaking havoc in our world. We never knew that something so tiny could affect everything.

It has affected our economies, our schools, our businesses, our places of worship, our family life, our spending patterns, and our travels.

Large companies are struggling, and some have collapsed. Many small businesses have ceased to exist. Job losses are too numerous to count.

Wealthy and powerful nations have been brought to their knees.

On the other hand, God is too big for us to see. He created the heaven and the earth (Genesis 1:1). He too can influence everything. We should seek His influence and welcome it.

Let us pray for His presence in our educational pursuits, our business ventures, our family matters, and in our places of worship. He even wants to be included in our vacation plans (as soon as they can be made).

Unlike the new coronavirus, He wants what is best for us (Jeremiah 29:11). Welcome Him joyfully!

55

Giants

Giants are much larger than us. They are strong and imposing. They were never intended to be our roommates, our colleagues, or our peers. Giants were never meant to be entertained. They are scary by their very nature and cause us to run and hide in fear (1 Samuel 17:23-24). But they can be defeated.

The most well-known giant in the Bible was defeated by a shepherd boy (1 Samuel 17:49). Other giants were also slain by regular men (1 Chronicles 20:4-8). One giant was even a king (Deuteronomy 3:11).

Do we have giants in our lives today? Situations that seem insurmountable, issues that will not go away, and problems that resist all attempts at a solution?

There are giants of fear and anxiety, giants of sickness and disease, giants of worry and doubt, giants of poverty, giants of strife and conflict, giants of depression, and giants of unbelief and lack of faith.

Identify your giant. You will not defeat an enemy that has not been identified as such.

Launch a campaign against your giant. Giants are never defeated by accident. Thankfully, we have not been left at the mercy of our giants.

We have been given effective weapons. The Word of God is a powerful weapon, and so are prayer and fasting. Conquer your giant and be victorious.

56

Concern for others

Nehemiah worked in the palace in close contact with the king, but he never forgot his homeland, enquiring of its state.

When he heard disturbing news about Jerusalem (Nehemiah 1:3), he was devastated. He chose to get involved. Though in relative comfort in the palace, his heart ached for his homeland and its distress.

If we are comfortable, we should be concerned about others who are in distress.

Nehemiah served in a position of trust. God used his position to bring deliverance to Jerusalem. A low-ranking servant would not have had the clout and opportunity to request resources from the king (Nehemiah 2:7-8).

Be concerned about others and ask God to show you how you can help.

57

Blessed by Association

The blessings of the Lord were never meant to be contained within small areas or to single individuals or for short periods of time (Exodus 23:25, Numbers 10:32).

Isaac was blessed in a famine (Genesis 26:1,12). Israel was blessed in Goshen (Exodus 10:23).

The blessings on Obededom, after he received the ark into his home, were poured out on his household and his generations (2 Samuel 6:10-11). He had many sons and grandsons who became mighty men serving in the house of God (1 Chronicles 26:8).

When Jesus invited Himself to the house of Zacchaeus, the host was excited, welcoming Him gladly (Luke 19:5-6); for he did not belong to that group in society who could boldly invite Jesus to their home (Luke 7:36).

Zacchaeus and his household received the blessings of salvation. The entire community benefitted (Luke 19:8).

When we welcome Him, His presence, and His true servants gladly into our homes and hearts, blessings follow, not just for us, but for our families and our communities.

The jailer who took Paul into his home after the near prison break was saved, along with his family (Acts 16:25-34). Even the prisoners benefitted as his treatment of those under his care would have been impacted.

Cornelius welcomed Peter (Acts 10:24) and his family and friends received the blessing of the Holy Spirit. A woman of means welcomed Elisha into her home and was blessed for the rest of her life (2 Kings 4:17).

The blessings of the Lord upon us can be poured out on those around us. We have an awesome responsibility on our shoulders.

We pray for our families, our communities, and our nations.

58

Children

Psalm 127

Children are not meant to be a nuisance, a burden, or an inconvenience. They are a heritage of the Lord. They are to be properly trained (Proverbs 22:6), aimed in the right direction, and set on the correct path.

They can be compared to arrows, which no one deliberately shoots into the ground.

Apart from abortion being the murder of innocents, something God hates (Proverbs 6:17), and eliminating a potential temple of the Lord (1 Corinthians 3:16), this act also says to God: *"I do not want this gift and I am throwing it away."*

Human beings would be very offended if they gave you a gift and you threw it away, not even giving it to someone else.

Maybe the experts who would have come up with cures, treatments, and vaccines for diseases plaguing the world today were discarded 20 or 30 years ago.

How many skilled musicians, singers, scientists, researchers, and artists have been flushed away, washed away, or left to die unattended.

May God have mercy on us.

59

Waiting Required

Psalm 40:1; Isaiah 40:31

No one likes to wait. Whether it is in a restaurant, a bank, government office, clinic, or at a bus stop, waiting is no fun. Waiting for medical attention can be distressing. Waiting for our investments to pay off and waiting to be appreciated can be frustrating.

Motorists are agitated waiting for the light to turn green. Many husbands in particular can speak of waiting for their wives to get ready to go out. Some of us get annoyed while waiting on the microwave.

Waiting on the Lord can be frustrating, too. For while we are waiting, we know He is able, and nothing is too hard for Him (Genesis 18:14). We know that time is not an issue for Him (Joshua 10:13), for He made time and will end time (Genesis 1:14; Revelation 10:6).

Yet He keeps us waiting. Why?

Abraham waited for the son of promise (Genesis 21:2).

Joseph waited for his freedom (Genesis 41:14).

In Egypt, the children of Israel waited for deliverance (Exodus 3:7-9).

Elisha waited for his double portion (2 Kings 2:9).

The parents of John the Baptist waited (Luke 1:5,20).

The apostles waited for the Holy Spirit (Acts 2:1).

Paul, then Saul, waited to receive his sight (Acts 9:8-9).

The church is awaiting the return of our Lord (Matthew 24:44; 1 Thessalonians 4:16).

In fact, the whole planet is waiting (Romans 8:22).

So, while we wait, we are never alone and are in good company.

Waiting builds character.

Waiting renews trust.

Waiting strengthens faith.

Waiting keeps us focussed on Him.

"Wait on the LORD: be of good courage, and he shall strengthen thine heart: wait, I say, on the LORD." (Psalm 27:14).

60

Nehemiah

Nehemiah chapters 1 - 13

Nehemiah was a man of prayer and a man of action. He repented on behalf of his people and sought the intervention of God before he petitioned his boss, the king. He recognised with whom all power lay.

He did research, set timelines, sourced aid, and carefully planned his project. The project, the rebuilding of the wall of Jerusalem, was not a selfish one but was for the benefit of the nation and the people of God. He was never enticed by monetary gain.

He expertly managed human resources. Priests, Levites, rulers, tradesmen, and ordinary men and women worked on the project.

He faced a lot of opposition from start to finish, but he had a genuine concern for the work of God and for the people of God, sacrificing personal comfort.

Nehemiah sought to lead the people in the ways of God and was not satisfied to simply allow ills to continue. He did not ignore wrongs in society and among the people of God, but bravely tackled and challenged the status quo.

He was fearless as he upbraided wrong-doers and removed corruption. Even when his personal safety was under threat, he relentlessly continued in the work of the Lord. The land had revival.

In addition to lengthy prayers, the book of Nehemiah is sprinkled with short, powerful prayers. Long, flowery prayers are usually ineffective as they are designed to impress human hearers (Luke 18:11).

Let us follow the example of Nehemiah. Pray constantly (Luke 18:1), be fearless in the work of the Lord (2 Timothy 4:2), and persist in spite of opposition, no matter its source and level of organisation. The work of the Lord must continue (John 9:4).

Let us pray for all leaders (1 Timothy 2:1-2).

61

Skip to the Good Part

2 Chronicles 5

Whether it is a book, a movie, or a tour, we like to skip the minor details and get to the good part.

When Solomon dedicated the temple, the priests could not stand to minister, for the glory of the Lord filled the structure. In our churches and in our lives, we crave that level of His presence. But we need to note what went on before.

Solomon and the children of Israel had done all they could. The temple was built according to plan, dedicated vessels were in place, numerous sacrifices were offered, the ark was brought in the way God commanded, the priests and Levites were sanctified and there was unity in the worship.

The Levites were clothed in white linen, a mode of dress linked to holiness and the presence of God (Daniel 10:5; 12:7; Revelation 19:8,14).

There were 120 priests blowing trumpets, instruments associated with His presence (1 Thessalonians 4:16; Revelation 8:6). In the Upper Room, there were 120 disciples (Acts 1:15). The unity in the temple praise and worship was similar to the unity in the Upper Room (Acts 2:1).

Then the cloud descended.

We are His temple (1 Corinthians 3:16). We need to dedicate ourselves, live according to His plan, and be unified in purpose to have more of Him in our lives.

There was pure gold, silver, and precious stones in the temple, but all were eclipsed by His glory. May His presence be the most outstanding element in our lives so that other things fade away.

62

Still He Loves Us

If some of our friends knew <u>everything</u> about us:
- Our background
- Our problems
- All our acts
- All our thoughts

they may reconsider the friendship, with good reason. But God:
- knows us before we are born (Jeremiah 1:5; Psalm 139:13)
- sees our struggles (Mark 6:48)
- knows our thoughts (Matthew 9:4; Hebrews 4:12)
- knows our 'secret' sins, mistakes, things we regret now or will regret later (2 Samuel 11:27)

Still:

He loves us (John 3:16; Jeremiah 31:3), forgives us (2 Samuel 12:13), and wants a relationship with us (Revelation 3:20).

What does He expect from us?
- Our love (Deuteronomy 6:5; 1 John 4:19)
- Our worship (Psalm 107:21; John 4:24)
- Our obedience (Deuteronomy 5:32; James 1:22)

63

Inner Cleansing Required

Pride, hatred, jealousy, and prejudice destroy from the inside out unless they are dealt with. It is possible to have these operating in our lives and not be aware of them. That makes them dangerous.

It could be the way we were brought up, the remnants of some former beliefs, or the result of past experiences and accomplishments. Whatever the origin, these have no place in the people of God.

We need to consecrate ourselves to Him and receive the cleansing that only comes to a life completely surrendered to Him.

In the Bible, there are many examples of persons who were destroyed because of pride, hatred, jealousy, and prejudice.

- King Saul (1 Samuel 18:8; 31:4)
- King Uzziah (2 Chronicles 26:16,19)
- Haman (Esther 3:5-6; 7:10)
- Pharaoh (Exodus 5:2; 14:28)
- Goliath (1 Samuel 17:4,50)

The brothers of Joseph envied him (Genesis 37:4-11). Christ was envied by religious authorities (Mark 15:10). Paul was envied by unbelieving Jews (Acts 17:5).

Even some of the apostles and early disciples had to rid themselves of the prejudice to which they were prone (Acts 10:15,45).

    Let us not fall victim to these.

64

Decision Time

It seems so easy to grasp, yet we keep stumbling over it: **Stay close to God and He will stay close to us. Seek Him and find Him** (2 Chronicles 15:2; James 4:8).

God does not appreciate being treated as a hotel bell boy:

- Just ring the bell and He will pop up and do our bidding.
- Otherwise, He should keep out of sight or stand in a corner and not get involved in our lives; have no influence on us.
- Remain unseen unless summoned.

He is not our spare tyre, our first-aid kit, our emergency flash-light, nor our hurricane shutters.

God is <u>not</u>: *For emergency use only*.

What type of relationship do we want with Him?

We decide.

65

The Talking Donkey

Numbers 22

The children of Israel were on the move, conquering as they went. The king of Moab was afraid. He decided to fight them with a spiritual weapon and sought to hire the prophet Balaam to curse them. He sent elders to the prophet.

God told Balaam that the people they wished him to curse were actually blessed. In other words, God said, **No, do not go with them.**

The king did not give up. He sent a higher-ranking delegation to the prophet, with promises of greater rewards.

The prophet at first protested, but by entertaining the men and waiting to hear from God, he was telling God that His first response was not acceptable. God allowed him to go with them and he saddled his donkey.

Mistakenly, the prophet took this to mean that God approved. Not because God allows us to do something means that He approves.

The Lord sent an angel with a sword to slay the prophet. The angel was visible to the donkey, but not to the prophet. Three times the donkey saw the angel and saved the prophet's life by veering out of the way, but the prophet was unaware and punished the beast.

The Lord opened the mouth of the donkey. The prophet was still clueless and proceeded to carry on a conversation with the animal. A prophet who communicated with

God was now talking to a donkey.

When you are outside the will of God, you can find yourself in embarrassing situations. The prophet was so blinded by greed, pride, and a sense of his own importance, that a donkey had better vision than him.

God can use the rejected, the not-so-smart, or the most unlikely. Remain in His will and be safe.

66

God of Abundance

Our God is a God of abundance!

Just look at the stars in the night sky and the grains of sand on the beaches.

God is not a God of drops, trickles, or sprinkles. He is a God of gushing waters (Numbers 20:11; John 7:38).

He is the God of the overflowing and the overwhelming.

How big is your problem now?

67

Deliverance

"The angel of the L<small>ORD</small> encampeth round about them that fear him, and delivereth them." (Psalm 34:7)

In wildlife documentaries, we often see predators capturing and devouring prey.

The camera crew makes no attempt to intervene and save the life of the hapless animal. They are not there to disturb nature, and after all, predators need to eat.

Good for us that the angel of the Lord is not with us for observation or recording purposes. We are delivered.

PRAISE THE LORD!

68

Precious Life

You are precious in the sight of the Lord. If some try to belittle you, call you worthless, make you feel less than a man or less than a woman, you remain His child. He paid a big price for us all (Romans 5:8).

On election day, all votes are equally valuable. There are no superior or inferior votes. In the same way, all souls are equally precious. Christ died for us all.

Genius or challenged, rich or poor, cherished or scorned, surrounded by loved ones or all on your own, the love Christ has for us is the same (John 3:16).

Maybe life treated you unfairly, maybe you made unwise decisions, or maybe you feel everyone is against you. Remember He loves you and desires a relationship with you.

Make Him the Lord of your life today, if you have not done so before. Be assured of a brilliant eternal future.

Father in the name of Jesus, forgive me of all my sins. Thank You for loving me and accepting me into Your Kingdom. AMEN.

69

Lies, Lies

There are lessons to be learnt from Ananias and Sapphira, the lying duo (Acts 5:1-11).

God does not tolerate lies.

- He does not appreciate pretence, which is a form of lying.
- The true servants of God often see beyond what our human eyes see.

Those were the days of the early church. The Holy Spirit had recently been poured out. Surely, our modern times are different. But has the power of the Holy Spirit diminished over time? Are His servants less empowered? Has God become more accepting of lies and pretentious displays?

We all know those answers.

- Those who speak in His Name claiming to have received a message from Him when they have not (Jeremiah 23:21);
- Those who pretend to be living for Him but actually lead a double life (Ezekiel 8:12) and,
- Those whose sole interest is looking or sounding good, spiritually (John 12:6)…

… Are all liars

Fathers produce offspring. The devil is the father of lies. Anyone who persists in living a lying lifestyle is following in the steps of their father (John 8:44).

Among those denied entry into Heaven will be liars (Revelation 21:8).

No one wants to go to the other place but there are only two options.

70

Well Done

Some of us work hard to hear the words *"well done"* from a senior, a colleague, or from someone we respect and admire.

We feel a sense of pride and accomplishment. All the effort and hard work paid off. It was not in vain.

Imagine what it would be like to hear those words from our Lord.

"Well done, thou good and faithful servant: thou hast been faithful over a few things, I will make thee ruler over many things: enter thou into the joy of thy lord..." (Matthew 25:21)

Let us work together towards that goal.

71

In the Furnace

Daniel 3

The three Hebrew boys made a stand for the Lord, not knowing whether He would deliver them from the furnace or not. They were trusting Him whichever way it went. What faith!

Most of us have faith to believe that He would keep us out of the furnace, not walk around the furnace with us.

The Lord appeared in the furnace after they were thrown in, not that He was not present all along, but He showed Himself in a visible form. Even the initially unbelieving king recognised Him.

Surely, it did not have to reach that far. Our Lord could have extinguished the flames and chilled the heat before they were thrown in. The king could have changed his mind, for the heart of the king is in His hand (Proverbs 21:1).

But the three youths were destined for the furnace, as are many of us, who are destined for fiery trials (1 Peter 4:12).

Those young men were in the furnace, but they were not on their own. They had not been abandoned. They were not in a hopeless situation and neither are we.

We may be in a fiery place because of our stand in Him. Do not lose hope.

Those looking on and expecting us to perish will recognise His presence with us. Maybe we ourselves are wondering how we are surviving. It is because He is with us.

"... there is no other God that can deliver after this sort." (Daniel 3:29)

72

Always Done

God told King Cyrus to build Him a temple at Jerusalem (2 Chronicles 36:23). Nehemiah heard of the distress at Jerusalem and prayed for guidance and favour from God in order to build the wall around Jerusalem (Nehemiah 1).

Sometimes God gives specific instructions and sometimes He empowers His servants to do His will, without specifically telling them what to do.

The will of the Lord is always done, regardless of the opinion, personal preference, or agendas of man (Isaiah 55:11). Jesus even prayed about this (Matthew 6:10). Jonah was sent to Nineveh without his approval (Jonah 1). He went, eventually.

Jeremiah was instructed to speak to the people of God (Jeremiah 1:5). Their response was not favourable since what he had to say was not pleasant. He tried to stop but could not (Jeremiah 20:9).

God did not instruct David to build a temple (1 Chronicles 17:6) but was pleased that he had the thought (1 Kings 8:18).

The work and will of the Lord will always be done despite obstacles. The wall around Jerusalem was quickly built (Nehemiah 6:15), while the temple was delayed for many years (Ezra 4:24) but was eventually completed (Ezra 6:15).

Whatever the circumstances, the will of God prevails.

73

On the Inside

There are times in life when the unexpected happens. I am not talking about the bad stuff, the things we dread, like the loss of a loved one, accidents, divorce and separation, onset of disease, and so on. I mean the good stuff, the unexpected blessings.

Obededom (1 Chronicles 13), had never planned to have the ark in his home. He had not reserved a space for it when he was building his house.

On the day the ark came into his home, he had not been eagerly awaiting its arrival. Yet, here it was. The ark!

A man had just lost his life. A time of celebration had been cut short.

With a sense of urgency, the ark was placed in a house. The prevailing atmosphere outside was one of fear, disappointment, apprehension, and anger. Yet Obededom enjoyed the presence of God in his home and received tremendous blessings.

The atmosphere outside did not influence what was happening inside his house. He and his family prospered despite what had happened before.

In this time of fear and apprehension, we too can enjoy the blessings of the Lord. His presence is with us in our homes; that makes the difference. Whether we are on lockdown, in quarantine, or are simply fearful, He is with us.

74

The Change

Ezekiel 37

Being in a low place, a valley, can be discouraging and depressing. Even more disheartening is being a very dry bone in a low place.

Examine the surroundings. Everyone is in the same position. There is no one who can help. All very dry bones in a low place, all disconnected, lacking power and purpose, merely existing in a solitary, sorry state for all to see.

It is so bad that not even the man of God knows if things can change.

But it can. The Word of God spoken over your life will remove reproach, cover you, cause unity, put you in your correct position in the Kingdom, and cause you to fulfil your purpose.

It will empower and strengthen so that the overall transformation will be so complete and so extreme that it will be widely known; only God could have done that!

75

The Homecoming

The ark of God finally arrived in its rightful place: the city of David. The trip home had been eventful.

It left behind a trail of disrupted lives, a broken god, disease, death, fear, anger, curiosity, and abundant blessings (1 Samuel 4-7; 1 Chronicles 13, 15).

Music, dancing, and the offering of sacrifices marked its homecoming. King David was jubilant. He blessed the people in the name of the Lord (1 Chronicles 16:2).

"And he dealt to every one of Israel, both man and woman, to every one a loaf of bread, and a good piece of flesh, and a flagon of wine." 1 Chronicles 16:3

Both men and women were treated equally, not the usual pattern for those days.

Each one received:

- A loaf of bread and a good piece of flesh symbolising the Son of God (John 6:51).
- A flagon of wine symbolising the Holy Spirit (Ephesians 5:18).

We, His children, all need the presence of God in our lives. We must receive His Son and welcome the Holy Spirit joyfully.

What a blessing!

76

Life Storms

Mark 4:36-41

Storms in life are usually sudden, unexpected, distressing, and unwelcome. While it is true that we are all on the same sea of life, we all face different storms at different times.

There are storms of sickness, storms of unemployment, storms of relationship and family matters, storms of disappointment and dashed dreams, financial storms, and storms of homelessness.

We can have more than one storm at a time. But our Lord remains Master of the wind and waves; they have to obey His command.

Worrying about the storms in our lives never impacts the storms. In fact, we are weakened while the storm continues to rage. We become stressed, fretful, and make poor decisions.

Some storms are more powerful than others, but all storms eventually weaken. Some storms last longer than others but no storm lasts forever.

We all desire smooth sailing, and we may get that sometimes, but when storms arise, we have to know what to do.

Do not wait until the storm starts to blow to intensify prayer life. Draw close to Him before the wind picks up speed and the waves grow big.

Sailing will not remain smooth, but we will know Who is in our boat and Who is on our side.

77

The Thief

"The thief cometh not, but for to steal, and to kill, and to destroy..." (John 10:10)

This pandemic seeks to steal our peace, our freedom, and our finances. To date, it has killed over two million persons around the world.

It has destroyed or severely damaged the travel industry, tourism industry, entertainment industry, and the restaurant industry, among others.

Economies that were experiencing growth have stagnated and declined. Further economic shrinkage is projected by some experts **BUT** God remains faithful.

We have no reason to doubt His faithfulness, His mercy, or His compassion (Lamentations 3:22-23).

We have an unfailing God standing up for us. While this world system is destined to fade away (Revelation 21:1), His Kingdom shall never end (Isaiah 9:7).

Let us keep faith, for He is not taken by surprise at recent events. He knew it was coming and how we would be impacted. We need to use this time to renew our trust.

Our God remains in control.

78

Revealing

Persons in their right mind do not go around revealing themselves to strangers or to those with whom no relationship exists. It is the same with the Lord.

Why should He reveal Himself to us when we refuse to spend meaningful time with Him, when we treat Him as a spare tyre, as a hotel bellhop, or as a first aid kit?

When God has revealed Himself to you, you bear an awesome responsibility (Exodus 24:9-10; Leviticus 10:1-2).

For to whom much is given, much is required (Luke 12:48).

79

War or Rest

Given the opportunity, most of us would choose rest rather than war. It would be lovely, though not realistic, if we could simply enjoy life free of turmoil, strife, and anxiety. But the truth is, some of us do not manage rest well (Nehemiah 9:28).

Life brings us battles. Sometimes, one after the other in rapid succession.

David was a warrior from his youth. He started off fighting predators that tried to snatch his sheep (1 Samuel 17:34-35) then a giant that threatened Israel (1 Samuel 17:4) and went on to fight numerous battles (1 Samuel 23:2; 27:8).

In contrast, his son, Solomon, was a man of peace. He had no wars because God gave him rest (1 Chronicles 22:9).

He had a huge task to perform. The first temple was waiting to be built. His father had made great preparation (1 Chronicles 22:5). That magnificent structure could not be put up while fighting. Wars would have been distracting, exhausting, and would have consumed resources required for the temple.

Nehemiah, on the other hand, built the wall around Jerusalem under constant threat of attack. It was so bad that the workmen were armed and ready for war while on the job (Nehemiah 4:18). The wall was finished in record time (Nehemiah 6:15).

We are all involved in building in the Kingdom of God. Whatever we are building, God has given us the material, the tools, the skill, and the right environment to do the job.

He is the Master Builder. Look at what He has built– the universe (Genesis 1:1), His Kingdom (Daniel 2:44; John 18:36), and His church (Matthew 16:18).

At war or rest, fulfil His purpose for your life.

80

For Want of Ten

For want of ten righteous persons, Sodom and Gomorrah were destroyed (Genesis 18:32).

Not that the ten would have negated the evil of the place, but the righteous presence of ten would have been enough for God to not utterly destroy them.

The prayer of a righteous man is valuable (James 5:16).

We must keep praying for our homes, our leaders, our communities, and our nations. Be one of the righteous!

Let not our land be destroyed for want of the prayers and presence of the righteous.

81

Kingdom Training and Preparation

Our Father trains and prepares us for our role in His Kingdom.

Moses would have received a first-class education in the palace of Pharaoh (Exodus 2:10). It was all in the plan of God. Moses had been chosen to lead Israel out of Egypt (Exodus 3:10), and also to write the first five books of the Bible (Deuteronomy 31:24), feats difficult to accomplish without the benefit of a superb education.

The Apostle Paul was bilingual and well educated. He was also a great speaker. Many books of the New Testament were written by him. He testified of Jesus and reasoned with public officials, governors, and kings (Acts 25).

Peter may have lacked that level of formal education, but he had the gift of oratory and was bold and vibrant. Even though it was a bit difficult for him to control himself at times (John 18:10), his bubbling personality and gift of speech served well in the Kingdom. On the day of Pentecost, with no sermon prepared, he delivered one that saw 3,000 converted (Acts 2:41). Also, following the miracle at the Gate Beautiful, he delivered a sermon *on the spot*, resulting in over 5,000 conversions (Acts 4:4).

Luke, the physician, wrote the book carrying his name, as well as the lengthy, detailed accounts of the book of Acts.

God has equipped you to do whatever He desires you to do. Though some things seem irrelevant, even burdensome, and grievous, you will be surprised how those skills and experiences will serve in good stead in His Kingdom.

We, of course, must make exception for the empowerment of the Holy Spirit on those like Gideon who feel inadequate (Judges 6:15).

Abraham was wealthy (Genesis 13:2), for he was to be the Father of many blessed nations. It would have been inappropriate for him to be poverty-stricken.

It is the Lord who orders our steps (Psalm 37:23).

82

To Make Great

What makes us great?

Is it our accomplishments, our wealth, our education, our careers, our political affiliation, the circumstances into which we were born, or our religious persuasion?

"... and in thine hand is power and might; and in thine hand it is to make great, and to give strength unto all..." 1 Chronicles 29:12

Our Lord is a complete package. In Him, everything is supplied. He is powerful and mighty. He makes great and gives strength.

"O LORD MY GOD, THOU ART VERY GREAT" Psalm 104:1.

83

Praise in the Wilderness

The journey through the wilderness was not easy for the children of Israel. This was new territory for them. Though they knew God was with them (Exodus 13:21) and they were going someplace better (Exodus 13:5), it was no fun trip.

The environment was dangerous. They never knew what to expect next and they did not know how long the trip would last. The lack of a correct attitude on their part actually caused a lengthening of the journey (Numbers 14:33).

They longed for certain aspects of their former lives and many times chose to murmur and rebel against the only One who could guarantee their safety. Their response to a new challenge was to complain. They neglected to praise, quickly forgetting the previous miracles of God (Psalm 78).

We are in a pandemic wilderness. This is new ground for us. It is not fun, but it is quite scary. We do not know how long it will last and what to expect next. Our lives have been completely changed. Everyone is affected.

However, we do know that God is with us and when we get through this wilderness, we should be in a better place in our prayer lives, our devotion, our faith, and our belief in His Word.

In a desolate and dangerous environment let us trust Him more. When we feel the urge to murmur and complain, let us praise.

It is a sacrifice (Hebrews 13:15), but it brings victory

(2 Chronicles 20:22; Acts 16:25). For He dwells in the praises of His people (Psalm 22:3).

84

Eagle or Grasshopper

Eagles fly high.

Eagles build their nest high.

Eagles soar above the issues that bother those at lower levels.

When trouble comes, it is time to go higher.

Grasshoppers operate close to ground level. They have a different perspective. They are affected by many things around them.

Grasshoppers are easy prey. They can be crushed without much effort.

With all the trouble in the world today, we need to go higher.

Be an eagle (Isaiah 40:31); not a grasshopper (Numbers 13:33).

85

Please Him

King Solomon married the daughter of Pharaoh, though the Lord had instructed otherwise (Exodus 34:12-16). She was just one of his strange wives (1 Kings 11:1).

However, he did not want her to live anywhere near the ark, for it represented the Holy presence of God (2 Chronicles 8:11).

Why enter a union of which God does not approve?

Why engage in acts that we know are not pleasing to God?

Well, they may bring instant pleasure or make us part of a popular movement.

Whether in youth or in old age, at home or abroad, all alone or with great company, in riches or in want, a servant or a supervisor, seek to please Him.

"And whatsoever ye do in word or deed, do all in the name of the Lord Jesus, giving thanks to God and the Father by him." Colossians 3:17

86

Hearts are Set

Under the leadership of Jeroboam, the northern part of Israel fell into idolatry (1 Kings 12:28). It would worsen as the years went by.

However, those who desired to worship the true God had to travel to Jerusalem to do so. No doubt, that decision found no favour with the leadership or with most of the population.

"...such as set their hearts to seek the Lord God of Israel came to Jerusalem..." (2 Chronicles 11:16)

When we set our hearts to seek God, it may not be popular or convenient. It may require great effort and it may actually seem easier to do whatever everybody else is doing.

Some resort to evil because they refuse to seek the Lord (2 Chronicles 12:14).

But there are rewards for a decision to seek the Lord and those rewards are paid both in this life (Psalm 9:9,10) and in the one to come (Revelation 22:12).

May we, even in these troubling times, set our hearts to seek the Lord.

87

Our Hope

We are stressed and confused. These times are troubling. We grapple with lost jobs, closed schools, decreased incomes, reduced economic activity, spent savings, fear of disease, and isolation.

We are affected socially. For months, some of us have not seen our friends face to face. Hugs, kisses, and even handshakes, are things of the past. Some, living with domestic abuse and violence, have no escape. Many are suffering mentally. Others are putting on a brave face trying to ride it out.

Our travel plans have been smashed. Weddings have been either postponed or scaled down. Even funerals have not escaped as we bury our dead, practically isolated, without the support of friends and family. Young children are growing up in a strange world, living in a new normal.

It seems as if everything has shown itself to be unstable. Yet, He remains stable (Hebrews 13:8). He shows no sign of being shaky or on the verge of collapse. He has never depended upon man and his institutions for His existence.

He has not abandoned us and has no intention of so doing (Matthew 28:20). We do not know what the future holds in store for the economies of the world, but we know He is the Creator and Ruler of this universe (Colossians 1:16).

Rest in Him. Trust in Him. He is still God. He has not

lost power. He is not stressed or confused. This is the time for us to remain close to Him.

None of us are unaffected by this pandemic. It has touched us all in one way or another. What should we do?

KEEP TRUSTING!!

88

A Perfect Heart

King Amaziah came to the throne of Judah following the assassination of his father (2 Chronicles 24, 25). The latter years of his father's reign were marked with idolatry, martyrdom of the Lord's servant, military invasion, and defeat.

Amaziah ascended to the throne doing what was right in the sight of the Lord; it seemed as if all was well (2 Chronicles 25:2). However, though his actions appeared spiritually correct, his heart was not perfect towards God.

Later, he turned to worship the idols of a nation he had conquered, ignored the Word of God, challenged the king of Israel to battle and was sorely defeated. His house and the temple were looted, part of the wall of Jerusalem was broken down, citizens were carried away as hostages, and he was later assassinated. An unfortunate train of events was put into play because of the condition of his heart towards the Lord.

It is not just what we do and how it appears to others; the state of our heart towards God is most important, for He sees it (Hebrews 4:12), and it determines our future actions and our destiny.

89

Prophet, Priest, and King

He is the Prophet about whom Moses spoke (Deuteronomy 18:15).

He is our Great High Priest (Hebrews 4:14).

He was born King (Matthew 2:2) and is the King of Kings (Revelation 19:16).

He is the only Prophet, Priest, and King.

Moses was a prophet. He was of the tribe of Levi, later chosen to be priests and he ordained the first priests (Leviticus 8:6), but he had no royal blood.

Samuel was a prophet from a young age (1 Samuel 3:20), performed priestly duties (1 Samuel 7:17), but never aspired to be king. In fact, he warned Israel about their desire for a king and was grieved that they even had that desire (1 Samuel 8:6).

David was a mighty king, and his writings are full of prophecy (Psalm 22:1; Psalm 34:20), but he was never a priest, and highly respected that office (1 Samuel 22:21).

King Uzziah was severely punished for attempting to perform priestly duties (2 Chronicles 26:16).

Elijah was a prophet and at times functioned as a priest (1 Kings 18:30) but was no king.

The role of Jesus as a Prophet, Priest, and King remains unchallenged and will stay that way. He is never grouped with others.

OUR PROPHET, PRIEST, AND KING.

90

The Choice

1 Kings 18:21

Following the Lord is a choice. That decision is not forced on anyone. If one decides not to follow, that is also a choice. Each choice brings with it benefits and consequences in this life and the next.

Among the benefits of following the Lord are a likelihood of a longer, healthier life, decreased risk of making poor lifestyle choices, and a likeliness to live free of guilt. It is not that followers of the Lord have no challenges, but they should know where to turn for help.

Nothing can surpass the eternal benefit of serving the Lord in this life. For we get to spend eternity with Him in Heaven.

The choice to not follow the Lord has consequences too. There is an increased chance of contracting diseases associated with sexual promiscuity and substance abuse. Guilt arising from past actions and stresses associated with unforgiveness are also likely to be issues.

The afterlife consequence overrides it all though, for eternal separation from God awaits in Hell.

Make the right choice today. Serve Him!

91

Restoration

A time of loss is always grievous and hurts deeply.

Restoration from the Lord may come soon after the loss, or it may take a while. Whichever way it occurs, restoration does not just return what you lost. There is always something extra.

Abraham, then Abram, went after the enemy that had captured his nephew and his possessions, along with several others (Genesis 14). He returned victorious with the people and goods. However, on his return, he met Melchizedek, King and Priest, who served him bread and wine and blessed him. Abraham gave him tithes of all. This was a spiritual blessing that has come down to us. We have the institutions of communion and tithes.

The loved ones of David and his men had been taken captive by the Amalekites (1 Samuel 30). After a time of weeping and of blame-throwing, David enquired of the Lord and pursued the abductors. David and his men recovered all. In addition, they took flocks and herds. That was the extra.

After his troubles, the Lord gave Job twice as much as he had before (Job 42:10).

The children of Israel were in captivity in Babylon for 70 years because of idolatry. The new conqueror, King Cyrus, was instructed by God to rebuild the temple at Jerusalem (2 Chronicles 36:23; Ezra 1).

Captives were free to return home to accomplish the

task. The vessels that had been looted from the temple of God and placed in a temple of a false god were returned. But there was extra. Those around them donated gold, silver, and animals for the work.

In this difficult time of financial and emotional loss for us, let us pray for restoration and the extra that comes with it.

92

Priority

2 Chronicles 28, 29

As a boy, Hezekiah saw the actions of his father, who adopted foreign false gods, refusing to worship the true God.

He sacrificed his son (2 Kings 16:3) and paid other kings to help him fight off enemies sent by God. Those kings caused him more distress.

His enemies were strong against him, he assumed, because of the gods they worshipped, so he purposed to worship them as well.

He built altars all over Jerusalem in honour of strange gods and even closed down the temple. More trouble came as he drifted further and further from God.

When Hezekiah came to the throne, there was much to be done, but one thing burned in his mind. For in the first year of his reign, in the first month, he re-opened the temple, gathered the Levites and priests, and instructed them to sanctify themselves.

Following that, they cleansed the temple and sanctified the vessels. The king assembled the people in worship, set the Levites in position with their instruments, and offered sacrifices to God.

That was his priority. He did it as soon as he got the opportunity. Some of us have time and opportunity that we lacked before.

What is our priority?

93

Bring the Book

There are cases in the Bible where the Book of the law of Moses was uncovered or brought out and read to the people after years of neglect (2 Chronicles 34:14; Nehemiah 8:1).

After it was read, things changed. King Josiah led his people in repentance and in keeping the feasts of the Lord (2 Chronicles 35). Weeping, then rejoicing resulted when Ezra read the words of the Book to the people (Nehemiah 8:9-10).

Kings had been instructed to read the Book daily (Deuteronomy 17:19). Most of them never did but led their people into idolatry. One king even threw it into the fire (Jeremiah 36:23). However, two kings, David and Solomon, contributed to the Book by writing God's Word. Priests were responsible for keeping the Book (Deuteronomy 31:9; 24-26).

We are kings and priests (Revelation 1:6). What are we doing with the Book, His Word?

These are not simply words printed on paper. The Book is alive, and it is powerful (Hebrews 4:12). We are supposed to speak it and meditate upon it (Joshua 1:8), but to do that, we first have to read it.

It guides us (Psalm 119:105), prospers our way (Joshua 1:8), and keeps us from sinning (Psalm 119:11).

94

No More Delays

The enemies of the Jews had successfully disrupted the construction of the second temple at Jerusalem for many years (Ezra 4:23-24). Even the people of God themselves gave up on the project (Haggai 1:2). Then the Word of the Lord was spoken by His prophets and construction resumed (Ezra 5).

Their enemies were enraged. They went to the construction site demanding to know who had given authorisation and also requested the names of the men involved in the project.

They wasted no time sending a letter to the king requesting that a search of the archives be carried out to see whether any former monarch had authorised this project.

A search revealed that King Cyrus had ordered the project, returned the temple vessels to the rightful owners, and provided financing (Ezra 6).

The reigning monarch ordered that the project be delayed no longer. Further, he instructed the detractors that from taxes collected, they should supply building materials and items required for the daily sacrifice.

These things were to be done with haste. For the king realised that the prayers offered in the temple would benefit him and his sons.

There would be deadly consequences for anyone who persisted in obstructing the project. No voice could be raised in opposition. The king had spoken!

Well, The King has spoken over us and our families. What the enemy meant for evil, GOD, our King forever, has turned it around for our good (Genesis 50:20).

95

Our Father Abraham

Children inherit certain characteristics from their fathers. Whether these are desirable or not is another matter.

Our spiritual father, Abraham, was a great man of faith (Hebrews 11:8), though, like all humans, he had his weak points (Genesis 12:13; 16:2).

Abraham:

- Obeyed God (Genesis 12:1).
- Was a peacemaker (Genesis 13:8).
- Defended his family (Genesis 14:14).
- Believed God even when it looked absurd (Genesis 15:6).
- Was hospitable (Genesis 18:2).
- Interceded before God for others (Genesis 18:23).
- Made provision for all his children (Genesis 17:18; 25:5-6).
- Organised his estate before his death, so that there would be no disputes after his passing (Genesis 25:5-6).

Today, the spiritual and biological descendants of Abraham are all over the world, exerting great influence.

May we emulate the characteristics of our Father, Abraham.

96

The Real Trouble

In this pandemic climate of fear, financial woes, and uncertainty, we all have trouble of one kind or another.

It seems that the enemy has been sending it specially packaged with our names written on it. For he still seeks those whom he can devour (1 Peter 5:8).

But think about it; our lives last a very short time (Psalm 103:15), compared to eternity. Let us make sure that our hearts are right with the Lord.

We wonder when normalcy will be restored, and when we will be able to resume our regular lives with its normal issues.

While no one has the answers to these concerns, we do know that our God has not been dethroned (Psalm 103:19) and that He still loves us (1 John 4:9).

Remember what is really important. It is not just how we weather this present crisis, but where we spend eternity.

97

Determination

"And Solomon determined to build an house for the name of the Lord, and an house for his kingdom." (2 Chronicles 2:1)

Solomon's father, David, had made great preparation to build the temple but was not allowed to do so (1 Chronicles 28:3). Instead, the task would fall to Solomon (1 Chronicles 28:10).

David had given towards the project and inspired the congregation to do the same (1 Chronicles 29). He had made arrangements for administrative support, raw materials, and labour (1 Chronicles 22). He even gave the plan for the design of the building to Solomon (1 Chronicles 28:11).

All was set. However, it was still up to Solomon. He could have chosen to use those resources selfishly but was on board with the project. He determined to build the temple.

We receive gifts from the Lord, and He has given us abundant resources. We also benefit from godly counsel, encouragement, teaching, and prayer, but we still have a choice to make.

People can determine to do all sorts of things with God-given gifts, but what are we determined to do with what He has given us?

May we use His gifts to build His Kingdom.

Solomon followed the plan for the temple faithfully.

May we follow His plan for our lives, for we are His temple (1 Corinthians 3:16).

98

Eyes Right

Hebrews 12:2

In a parade, when the command *'eyes right'* is shouted, no marcher gazes straight ahead, at the crowd, the photographers, or their fellow marchers.

All eyes are focussed on the one who is judging the parade or on the one in whose honour the event is being held.

Well, the command has been issued to us.

Eyes on Jesus, not on the waves.

Eyes on the One who is mighty to save.

Do not focus on the pandemic.

Or on the enemy and his gimmicks.

Focus on the Creator.

Focus on our Saviour.

Eyes right, on the One who is The Light.

PRAISE THE LORD!

99

No Other

God, like no other (Exodus 15:11).
King, like no other (Matthew 2:2).
Lord, like no other (John 20:28).

Mediator, like no other (1 Timothy 2:5).
High Priest, like no other (Hebrews 4:14).
Shepherd, like no other (John 10:14).

Provider, like no other (Philippians 4:19).
Healer, like no other (1 Peter 2:24).
Friend, like no other (Proverbs 18:24).

Creator! There is no other (Genesis 1:1).
Saviour! There is no other (Acts 4:12).
Redeemer! There is no other (1 Peter 1:18).

100

Nehemiah, the Wall Builder

Nehemiah 4 and 6

The Jews in Jerusalem were in a state of reproach. Their city wall was broken down. Their enemies rejoiced until Nehemiah arrived with the authority of the king behind him.

Sanballat and Tobiah, enemies of Jerusalem, featured prominently as work on the wall started. Sanballat, in anger, mocked the Jews in public. Tobiah described their work as being so inconsequential that a fox could quickly demolish it.

Wall construction progressed and the number of opponents and the intensity of their rage grew. They planned both open warfare and secret ambush, but all their plans failed.

The response was prayer and active preparation and strategy for battle while continuing to work. As construction continued, the attacks escalated. The aim of the enemy was to stop the project at all costs. Now the enemy shifted strategy. They pretended to desire peace, setting up a meeting, but Nehemiah was able to discern the true motives.

Next, they sent Nehemiah a letter, accusing him of planning a rebellion and threatening to report him to the king. That plan also failed. Nehemiah was the victim of ridicule, lies, and death threats, not for personal reasons, but because he was leading the people of God in His work.

Finally, they enlisted the help of a hired prophet. They hoped Nehemiah would accept the words of the prophet as the words of God. Nehemiah did not. That was the final desperate attempt, for the wall was soon completed.

The attacks of the enemy are numerous and vary from scorn, open hatred, and pretence, to acts appearing to have the approval of God. In spite of attacks launched against us, let us continue in the work of the Lord.

101

Think Again

After King Hezekiah had sought the Lord, cleansed the temple, restored worship, sacrifices, and observance of the feasts of the Lord (2 Chronicles 29-31), up comes the king of Assyria into Judah. He eyed the fenced cities, surrounded them, and thought to win them for himself (2 Chronicles 32:1).

Fenced cities represented quite a trophy. A lot of resources had gone into their establishment; now they seemed very attractive. They did not belong to him. He had made no contribution to their establishment, but he thought to win them for himself.

In our world today, there are persons who view with envy the possessions and accomplishments of others. They have not made any contribution, but they want them for themselves. The objects, structures, or achievements may represent the combined efforts of generations or of several individuals, but someone out there decides that they want it for themselves, now.

You worked hard on raising your children, building your marriage, setting up your business, building your home, purchasing a vehicle, shepherding a flock, and some intruder or invader is thinking of winning them for himself.

Be it bad company, a homewrecker, a bandit, or a wolf in sheep's clothing, their aim is the same, i.e., to claim what is not theirs for themselves.

God protected Hezekiah and his land. We pray for His

protection upon us, our land, and what He has given us in the Name of Jesus.

102

Filled

He made the heavens and He filled them with planets, asteroids, moons, and more stars than we can count.

He made the earth and He filled it with air, trees, plants, animals of various kinds, and treasure.

He made the oceans, rivers, and lakes, and He filled them with amazing creatures, plants, and more treasure.

He made man and filled him with a desire to seek Him, to praise Him, and to worship Him.

He told man and woman to fill the earth (Genesis 1:28), but we have filled it with violence, corruption (Genesis 6:11), prejudice, and hatred.

We pray to be filled with His Holy Spirit, for then we shall be filled with peace, joy, and love.

103

Bread in the Wilderness

The children of Israel were well-provided with bread in the wilderness (Exodus 16:15). It was not the food they would have chosen for themselves (Numbers 11:5), but it was what was good for them.

They soon grew weary of the God-provided food and yearned after the foods of Egypt, the way we sometimes despise what God has provided and wonder why He did not do better.

Bread is the most basic of human food. Jesus, the Bread of Life (John 6:48), walked with His disciples, yet they were concerned with the availability and cost of bread to feed the multitude in a desert place (John 6:5-7).

Jesus fed the multitude with five loaves and two fishes. We, too, always concern ourselves with the temporal, and He provides that too, but our greater concern should be that we partake of the Bread that satisfies eternally.

Manna was temporary. It did not give everlasting life (John 6:49), but the Bread of Life offers so much more (John 6:58).

Man shall not live by bread alone (Deuteronomy 8:3).

God is a satisfier now, and in the life to come.

104

Water

Man, like the rest of nature, needs water to survive. It is a basic need. God provided water in the wilderness. It sprang out of a rock (Numbers 20:11). The children of Israel had no need to murmur about the lack of water. The Rock was there (1 Corinthians 10:4). The Lord knew they would need water in a dry environment.

The woman of Samaria (John 4) went to the well to draw water, but Jesus knew her thirst extended beyond that. She had had five husbands and other men in her life, but her thirst extended beyond that. She needed living water.

Her eyes were opened in that brief encounter at the well and she became a witness for the Lord.

He still calls the thirsty (John 7:37). He supplies not drops, sprinkles, and trickles, but rivers. He provides for our physical and spiritual needs. In a dry place, He is our fountain of life and His provision is not limited by the environment or by the economy.

GOD PROVIDES!

105

A Different God

How is our God different from other gods?

For the truth is, there are many other gods. They do exist and have followers and worshippers too.

Other gods keep their followers in fear constantly. They have to be careful to appeal to the relevant god for the prevailing situation. These gods need to be appeased and kept from getting angry. Who knows who will pay the price when these gods are angry?

Our God created the heavens and the earth. He sent His Son to die for our sins because He loves us beyond reason (John 3:16). He loves us tenderly, knows our names, and watches over us.

He forgives our sins and wants us to spend eternity with Him. He has a place prepared for us that is so amazingly lovely that we cannot imagine it (1 Corinthians 2:9). Our God is eternal, other gods are not (Revelation 22:13).

Our God does not tolerate the worship of other gods, and quite rightly so. Some try to worship the true God and others on the side. With our God, it is complete loyalty or none (Deuteronomy 5:7).

Choose to love and serve the true God while there is time. Love makes the difference.

106

King Uzziah

2 Chronicles 26

King Uzziah had made his way into a restricted area of the temple and was attempting to perform a duty outside the realm of his authority. King Uzziah crossed so many boundaries. He was not of the tribe of Levi and therefore did not qualify to minister in the temple. Further, only the descendants of Aaron were priests, and only they had access to the area where the altar of incense was located. The king was not supposed to be in that area, nor be in possession of the incense, much less approach the altar to offer it.

In the days of Moses, Levites had been chided for trying to elevate themselves to the priesthood (Numbers 16:6-10). No one except the sons of Aaron was to offer incense before the Lord (Numbers 16:40).

It is interesting that Uzziah did not set up idols nor dip his hands into the Lord's offerings. He did not chase women or adopt the lifestyle of the surrounding unbelieving nations, but he became proud. His heart was lifted up when he considered his many accomplishments. He made himself into an idol and he was challenging God on His law.

Had Uzziah been successful in this venture, a king of the tribe of Judah would have become a priest prematurely. That position was reserved for our Lord. Pride caused the downfall of Uzziah. He was smitten with leprosy while inside the Holy Place of the temple. He would spend the rest of his days isolated. His son assumed his duties.

We need to humble ourselves (1 Peter 5:6), for pride is a destroyer (Proverbs 16:18) and attracts the judgement of God (Daniel 4:37).

107

The Setback

When the children of Israel returned from captivity in Babylon, they set about building the temple at Jerusalem. God had told King Cyrus to build Him a temple at Jerusalem (Ezra 1).

The first thing they did was to record the ancestry of the former captives who were heading home after 70 years. This is when they realised that their ranks had been infiltrated, for some among them could not prove that they belonged to Israel. This problem even extended to the priesthood (Ezra 2:59-63). *Tares* (Matthew 13:25), were everywhere.

Upon arrival, they first set up the altar and offered sacrifices. They kept the feasts of the Lord (Ezra 3). We first need to restore our personal prayer lives before dealing with the entire assembly.

Then the foundation of the house was laid using donations, offerings, and funds provided by Cyrus. There was a great celebration when the foundation was completed. To the younger ones who had never seen the splendour of Solomon's temple, this was a great achievement. The elders, however, who knew the first temple, were overcome with emotion. It was a time of shouting for joy and weeping as memories were recalled.

Truth is, they should have never been in this position, for it resulted entirely from their idolatry and disobedience. How many of our troubles have been caused by our rebellion? We suffer setbacks because of this. It is best to keep following faithfully rather than try to bounce back from a major setback.

108

Still Blessed

King Balak of Moab, (Numbers 22), carried the prophet Balaam from one place to another hoping he would get a suitable vantage point from which he could curse the children of Israel (Numbers 23:13, 27).

But perspective or opinion does not matter; the people of God are blessed.

Only we can remove ourselves from the blessings of God. We can do this by disobedience and rebellion, just like the children of Israel. No enemy, neighbour, hired hand, or anyone else can remove us from the blessings of the Lord.

Even in a pandemic, we are blessed, though it may not look or feel like it. Let us ask Him to open our eyes so that we can see what we need to (2 Kings 6:17). If we are not seeing evidence of His blessing, it does not mean it is not there.

The blessing of God does not depend on our feelings nor on our day-to-day experiences. These may have us feeling down.

But God said we are blessed, and we hold onto that, no matter how difficult the times, how contrary the winds, or how violent the storm.

No matter how scary the pandemic, let us hold onto His promises. We have chosen life (Deuteronomy 30:19). We are blessed (Deuteronomy 28:2).

109

Not the Same

The start of construction of the temple at Jerusalem attracted a lot of attention (Ezra 4:1). The Jews, recently returned from captivity in Babylon, had a new respect, fear, and commitment to God. They had seen and lived the consequences of their refusal to serve the Lord.

As work commenced, the foreigners who had been brought into the land by the king of Assyria approached and offered assistance. They claimed to worship the same God as the children of Israel (Ezra 4:2).

Their response to the true God must have been similar to that of those foreigners who had been placed in Samaria; for they acknowledged the true God but continued to worship their false gods (2 Kings 17).

Now they were claiming to be the same and became quite upset when their offer of help and inclusion was refused. They actively disrupted the project for years, going so far as to write the king accusing the Jews of wrongdoing. They showed themselves to be the liars they really were. What was it that they sought to contribute?

When worshippers of other gods claim to be the same as worshippers of the true God, it may look and sound convincing. But it is not enough for persons to simply acknowledge the existence of God while continuing in the worship of other gods. Worship is a spiritual exercise.

There can be no dual worship.

110

King Saul

King Saul, the first king of Israel, habitually refused to obey God. He also sought to blame others for his errors. He never assumed responsibility and never genuinely repented (1 Samuel 13:11; 15:7-25).

Then he made it worse by consulting with a witch (1 Samuel 28:6-8). True, God was not answering him, but that was a hint for him to repent, not drift further away. He died for both these sins (1 Chronicles 10:13).

The blunders of Saul had far-reaching consequences for him, his generation, and his nation (2 Samuel 4, 21; 1 Chronicles 10).

- He died by his own hand and was lost for eternity.
- His assistant followed his lead.
- Three of his sons died in the same battle.
- The men of Jabesh, whom he had rescued early in his reign (1 Samuel 11), had to risk their lives to retrieve the bodies for burial.
- The burial was hardly fitting for the first king of Israel.
- The death of Saul and his sons in battle brought glory to a false god.
- Israel lost the battle.
- Israel also lost their inheritance, as they ran away from their cities and the enemy took possession.

- One son who reigned briefly was assassinated.
- Seven other sons were executed.
- The kingdom passed from his family to another.
- His young grandson became crippled for life when his nurse accidentally dropped him while fleeing.
- There was a lengthy famine.

Let us obey and be guided by Him.

111

Just Great

Great is the Lord (Psalm 104:1).

His Name is Great (Philippians 2:9).

His Power is Great (Isaiah 40:26; Matthew 28:18).

His Works are Great (Psalm 111:2).

His Mercy is Great (Psalm 108:4).

He is a Great King above all gods (Psalm 95:3).

He is a Great God (Psalm 77:13).

He is greatly to be Praised (Psalm 96:4).

GREAT IS THE LORD!

112

Reasons Why?

Why trouble comes?

- There are times when trouble comes upon us because of our own actions (Ezra 9:13; 2 Kings 4:39).

- Sometimes, it comes because of events in the spirit world (Job 1:12).

- Trouble may occur so that He has the opportunity to show His power in our lives (John 9:3; John 11:4).

- There are times when He is shifting us and things around us so that we would be in place for a great blessing (Genesis 50:20; Ruth 4:17).

- Trouble can occur because of our stand in Him (Jeremiah 18:18; Daniel 3:15).

Why He intervenes?

- Because of our faith and our prayers (Luke 5:12; Mark 5:23).

- Because He is touched by our pain (Luke 7:13-15; Mark 8:3).

- Because we actively seek Him and His deliverance (Mark 5:28; Matthew 15:28; 20:30; Luke 7:3).

- Because He wants to show His power to the unbelieving (Mark 3:5; Luke 13:11).

- Because there is a need to put things right (Luke 22:50-51).

- Because He wants to reward us for obedience (Luke 5:3-6).
- He acts in spite of our fear and unbelief (Matthew 8:26).
- He is fulfilling His Word (Micah 5:2; Luke 1:26, 27; 2:4).

No one likes trouble. Yet it comes to us all. In these times, it seems that everyone has trouble, some more than others. We have to know where to turn and Who is our help. Regardless of how it looks, our God is still on top of the situation (John 6:19).

Keep trusting!!

113

Impact

A chariot of fire complete with horses of fire separated the prophets Elijah and Elisha (2 Kings 2:11). Elijah, the older man, had completed his assignment. He was being taken up to Heaven in glorious fashion.

The younger prophet, Elisha, was about to commence on a powerful ministry, made even more so because of his dedication and persistence (2 Kings 2:2) and his service to the man of God (1 Kings 19:21).

The periods in which they ministered were not periods of cosy comfort but were filled with the power of God.

Both prophets performed numerous miracles, including resurrections; anointed, counselled, and rebuked kings; rid the land of false prophets; rescued widows; mentored junior prophets, and even influenced the outcome of wars.

The presence of a prophet of God is sure to make a great impact not only on the people of God but also on society as a whole, so that it would be widely known, there is a prophet in the land (2 Kings 5:8; 6:12).

114

The Inside Enemy

Tobiah was an active opponent of the rebuilding of the wall around Jerusalem (Nehemiah 4:3; 6:12). He married into Jewish society and was well connected to the nobles of Judah (Nehemiah 6:17). They tried to portray him in a good light to Nehemiah, who had been the victim of his verbal and other attacks.

The social connection was made stronger, for his son also married a Jew. Tobiah was tightly interwoven with the people of God but he remained an enemy.

When an enemy approaches from outside the ranks, he is easily identified and his attacks are anticipated. However, an enemy on the inside, who acquaints himself with our practices and who is well connected with those in leadership positions, is more difficult to spot and to fight.

Tobiah used his connections well, for the high priest prepared a special apartment for him in the temple. He was evicted by Nehemiah, recently returned to Jerusalem. The space reverted to its rightful use, which was the storage of temple vessels, tithes, and offerings (Nehemiah 13:7-9).

An inside enemy is dangerous, for he may be able to secure space, time, and other resources that really belong to God. These are an added advantage when launching attacks against the true servants of God and the work done in His Name.

Remember the teaching of Jesus about an enemy sowing weeds among the wheat. When Jesus returns, they will receive what they deserve (Matthew 13:30), but until then, they dwell among us.

115

Tune In

When I tune in to a radio station, that is what I hear.

When I switch to a television channel, that is what I see.

When I go surfing on the net, I choose which sites to visit and that is what I view.

When I go on social media, I choose my friends, put up my posts, and express my opinions.

When I choose to read, study, and meditate on the Word of God, that is what fills my mind, occupies my heart, influences my behaviour, and changes me from the inside out (Joshua 1:8; Psalm 119:105,162).

We ought to spend more time in His Word. It is a wonderful investment, sure to pay for years to come and the benefits extend into the next life.

116

Manna

God sent manna in response to a need (Exodus 16:15). He does not do anything just because He can, the way humans do. The children of Israel were in a barren place, the wilderness, and they needed supernatural provision.

Manna required some effort to collect. It did not fall directly in their tents or onto their laps. It also had to be prepared (Numbers 11:8). The provision of God will require some input from you, e.g. prayer, fasting, meditating on His Word, and helping others.

Manna did not seem outstanding in any way (Exodus 16:14). The most important thing about it was the fact that God provided it. Its appearance and taste did not seem to particularly impress the children of Israel (Numbers 21:5).

There were rules attached concerning when and how much could be collected (Exodus 16:16). Breaking the rules brought no profit and led to unpleasantness, as it went bad and bred worms (Exodus 16:20).

Manna was not *whenever* food or *forever* food; it had to be collected in the morning (Exodus 16:21). It ceased when they entered the promised land (Joshua 5:12) because other food was now available. Your blessings may be 'time relevant' and have conditions applied to them, the ignoring of which can lead to disaster.

117

Instruction

"Thou gavest also thy good spirit to instruct them..." Nehemiah 9:20

Unlike us, our God needs no guidance, counsel, or instruction (Isaiah 40:14).

The children of Israel in the wilderness were not left up to their own devices, for the Lord was there to give instruction and direction.

It was not always joyfully received or appreciated (Numbers 11:1), but they would not have survived without it.

We, too, cannot survive without His guidance, counsel, and instruction (Psalm 32:8; Isaiah 48:17).

118

Promotion

"For promotion cometh neither from the east, nor from the west, nor from the south. But God is the judge: he putteth down one, and setteth up another." (Psalm 75:6,7)

True promotion comes from the Lord.

God promoted Abraham from childless to Father of many nations (Genesis 15:3; Genesis 22:17).

God promoted Jacob from con man to Father of the tribes of Israel (Genesis 27:19; Genesis 32:28).

God promoted Joseph from slave to president (Genesis 37:36; Genesis 41:41).

God promoted Enoch and Elijah from earth to Glory (Genesis 5:24; 2 Kings 2:11).

God promoted Moses from fugitive to deliverer (Exodus 2:15; Exodus 3:10).

God promoted Joshua from servant to leader (Exodus 33:11; Joshua 1:2).

God promoted David from shepherd boy to king (1 Samuel 16:11; 2 Samuel 5:3).

God promoted Nehemiah from cupbearer to governor (Nehemiah 1:11; Nehemiah 8:9).

God promoted Peter and the others from fishermen to apostles (Mark 1:16; Revelation 21:14).

Haman was promoted by King Ahasuerus, but it proved to be his downfall (Esther 3:1; 7:10).

"The blessing of the Lord, it maketh rich, and he addeth no sorrow with it." (Proverbs 10:22)

119

Noah

Noah beat the odds. He lived a righteous life, in the midst of an unrighteous environment (Genesis 7:1).

In the eyes of the Lord, Noah stood out from those around him (Genesis 6:8).

God gave Noah a strange assignment. He was told to build a large vessel, an ark (Genesis 6:14). Noah did not live on the water. There was not even rainfall in those days (Genesis 2:6). He must have been the subject of ridicule and derision. In addition to him living a peculiar lifestyle and influencing his family to do the same, he was now building a strange-looking vessel.

Noah obeyed God (Genesis 6:22). His family was saved from destruction. He earned a place in the Faith Hall of Fame in the book of Hebrews chapter 11, verse 7.

Continue to serve God when those around you do not, or when they think you are strange and even make fun of you. It will pay off in the end.

120

Naturally Different

The people of God are supposed to be different (Esther 3:8), for they are sanctified or set apart (Hebrews 13:12).

Whenever the people of God are identical to those who do not know the Lord, we know something is wrong.

It is not that we deliberately set out to behave strangely; it is simply that the keeping of the law of God makes a natural distinction that is hard to miss.

We have no need to go out of our way to appear different; it happens on its own.

While Jesus walked the earth, it was not easy to tell Him apart from anyone else (Matthew 26:48; John 20:15), but time spent in His presence makes all the difference for His followers (Acts 4:13).

121

His Plan

We sometimes must abandon or alter our plans, no matter how well thought out. Unforeseen circumstances, changes in health, fortune, and the economy, can all cause a change of plans.

God never has to abandon or alter His plans because He has perfect knowledge (Isaiah 46:10; Colossians 2:3). It does not matter what happens; He is never caught off-guard or taken by surprise.

When man sinned in the Garden of Eden, He already had a plan (John 1:29; Revelation 13:8).

In addition to the plan of redemption, He also has personal plans for us (Jeremiah 29:11). His plan is for our benefit, unlike the plan of the enemy. And though we tend not to believe it, His plan is also better than our own plan.

May we surrender fully to His will.

122

Dilemma

When Esther and her people faced destruction (Esther 3), she could have:

- complained about how unfair life was;
- cried herself to sleep at nights;
- called a meeting of the leaders in the community and asked for their input;
- wished Haman dead;
- told her maids about her dilemma and sought their sympathy;
- pouted and sulked for days, or;
- withdrawn her enthusiasm

BUT, she prayed, fasted, and went to the king (Esther 4:16).

Esther would have accomplished nothing had she not entered the king's presence and made her petition known.

What do we do when we have more trouble than we can handle?

First, go to the Heavenly King, then go to the earthly king or whoever is in authority concerning the situation.

We have the right to seek the help of our Lord (John 14:14).

"It is better to trust in the Lord than to put confidence in man." (Psalm 118:8)

123

End Well

The reign of King Solomon was one of splendour, wealth, and opulence (Ecclesiastes 2:4-9). This was a man with the favour and blessings of God upon his life (2 Samuel 12:24).

He lived an extravagant lifestyle, even compared to other monarchs. He and his multitude of wives and concubines (he had over 1000 of them) would have required a lot of resources, both in materials and in labour.

He was such an imposing figure that there were no complaints during his lifetime. After his death, however, the people complained to the new king, his son. ***"Thy father made our yoke grievous..."*** (2 Chronicles 10:4)

Solomon had excelled in wisdom. God had appeared to him on more than one occasion (2 Chronicles 1:7; 7:12). His fame spread to nations far and near. Yet his desire for many unbelieving wives left a stain on his legacy (1 Kings 11:1-10; Nehemiah 13:26).

The temple built by him is still spoken of in awe; his reign was unique; his business ventures were successful; he outshone other monarchs; his wisdom was well known; he wrote three books of the Old Testament (1 Kings 4:32; 2 Chronicles 9); however, one weakness stands out.

For unlike his father David, who repented swiftly of his sin when confronted, the sin of Solomon snowballed in his old age (1 Kings 11:4). As a result, the nation of Israel was divided, with long-lasting consequences (2 Chronicles 10:19).

It is not enough for us to serve God well initially; we must end well or serve Him to the end of our days.

124

A Time to Run

There are times when we need to run.

Joseph, the husband of Mary, was told to flee to Egypt (Matthew 2:13) with Jesus and Mary. King Herod was trying to execute the Christ child.

Joseph, son of Jacob, fled from Potiphar's wife to avoid a sexually charged situation (Genesis 39:12).

A young prophet was sent by Elisha to anoint a new king over Israel (2 Kings 9:1-10). He anointed Jehu, gave him a message from the Lord, then opened the door and fled.

Whether you're running to remain faithful and avoid sin or to save your life, once you are a child of God, He is with you.

125

The Challenge

Unknown to Job, he was the subject of a challenge between the Lord and Satan (Job 1:6-12). Our names, lifestyle, and service to God are well known to the enemy. He believed Job loved God only because he was successful in his family life and in his business. God gave the enemy permission to strike these areas.

Job lost his employees, his business, his wealth, and finally, all his children. His response: **WORSHIP** (Job 1:20). That response must have caught the enemy by surprise. It was certainly not expected.

We would think that the enemy would have given up, admitted defeat, and moved on. But no, he is not the shy, retiring type. When we survive an attack of the enemy, it does not mean he has given up and will never attack again.

He presented himself again before the Lord (Job 2:1). In this encounter, it is again clear Who is in charge: *The One who asked for an account of the other's activities*. When you are struggling, remember Who is in charge.

The topic of Job again came up, but the enemy declared that a man would do anything, give anything, to save his body and his life. It is on this premise that kidnapping and abduction in our world are based. The enemy was given the green light to attack Job in his health, but he could not take his life (Job 2:6).

The health of Job rapidly deteriorated. He had already lost his children and his business. He was treated with scorn, his friends were shocked and did a miserable job of comforting him (Job 16:2), and his wife advised him to curse God and die (Job 2:9).

Job endured and was victorious in the end. He enjoyed restoration (Job 42:11-16).

Once the enemy is loose on this earth (Revelation 20), he will continue to launch attacks against the people of God. But we can be victorious, for our God is powerful.

www.ingramcontent.com/pod-product-compliance
Lightning Source LLC
Chambersburg PA
CBHW030907080526
44589CB00010B/191